Azrael
LOVES CHOCOLATE
michael's
A JOCK

Dedicated to Annie K., Ella K.,
Judy M., and The Rose.
You are forever in my heart.

ABOUT THE AUTHOR

Chantel Lysette is the creator and host of the highly acclaimed lecture/reading series, The Angel Galleries.™ She is also a double-certified Master of Usui Reiki (a form of intuitive energy healing), and has over a decade of instructional experience in meditative studies, intuitive studies, comparative world religion, and philosophical studies. She holds a BA in English with honors from Wayne State University (Detroit, MI).

©Britt Photographic

Azrael
Loves Chocolate

michael's
a Jock

An insider's guide to
what your angels
are really like

Chantel Lysette

Llewellyn Publications
Woodbury, Minnesota

First Edition
First Printing, 2008

Book design by Steffani Sawyer
Cover design by Gavin Dayton Duffy
Cover image © 2008 by iStockphoto
Interior illustrations © Jess Volinski / Visual Picnic
Llewellyn is a registered trademark of Llewellyn Worldwide, Ltd.

Library of Congress Cataloging-in-Publication Data
Lysette, Chantel.
  Azrael loves chocolate, Michael's a jock : an insider's guide to what your angels are really like / Chantel Lysette.—1st ed.
      p. cm.
  Includes bibliographical references.
  ISBN 978-0-7387-1441-7
  1. Angels—Miscellanea. I. Title.
  BF1623.A53L97 2008
  202'.15—dc22
                                           2008026613

Llewellyn Publications
A Division of Llewellyn Worldwide, Ltd.
2143 Wooddale Drive, Dept. 978-0-7387-1441-7
Woodbury, MN 55125-2989, U.S.A.
www.llewellyn.com

Printed in the United States of America

contents

—✝—

CONTENTS

ACKNOWLEDGMENTS

With deepest gratitude I wish to acknowledge:

The beautiful and benevolent hosts of the heavens for inspiring and guiding me to this moment, that I might share with all I encounter the compassion, love, and light that radiates through the universe and into the hearts of all living beings.

My dearest friend Jeremy Ponti for 2:00 AM reflections over coffee at the local diner that have led to many a lively discussion and spiritual discovery. Thank you for your tireless efforts and contribution to help bring this book to fruition.

The Earth angels that surrounded me with encouragement, offering their love and support: Debby Solomon, Jean Charette (Lex, I love you), Kim Britt, "The Ladies of the Rose," Melissa and Paul Ashbaugh, and the Jokinen family.

My clients, students, colleagues, and friends who have shared their lives and their angelic encounters with me, that we might all learn a bit more about the heavens ... and ourselves.

Llewellyn Publications for first inspiring me, when I was just an adolescent, to open my mind and heart to the vast wonders of the world, sparking my imagination and setting me upon a most magical journey that would lead me straight to this collaboration two decades later. Many, many thanks for this opportunity.

TESTING
SPIRITUAL WATERS

For centuries, angels have been portrayed in art and literature as sitting among clouds, bestowing blessings, wielding punishments, or appearing as luminous bodies to deliver messages from on high. Although angels have been intimately involved with us since day one, history has usually painted them simply as divine creatures who autonomously carry out God's will. While this is true in a sense, there is another side to the angelic realm—a side that few of us get to see. It's a side that can help us better connect with our companions in spirit, a side less focused on rituals and rites and more focused on each human being's personal relationship with the Divine.

In *Azrael Loves Chocolate*, I hope to take you on a fun ride through the angelic realms. My goal in this book is to reintroduce the archangels in a way that is familiar and tangible. I have focused on twelve archangels who, according to most religious texts, are the ones delegated to deal directly with humans and their affairs.

My lighthearted approach to the subject of angels may be a bit unorthodox, but it is not without purpose! At no time has there been a greater need to connect with the Divine than now, but what stands between us and the Divine are thousands of years of believing we are separate from God. The notion that the Divine resides only in the heavens, and humanity only here on Earth, erodes our kinship with our Creator. It is time to re-acquaint ourselves with the awe and beauty of this universe and those in charge of it—so what better way to begin than with a little humor? I see *Azrael Loves Chocolate* as a way to break the ice for many of us as we embark upon our spiritual journeys, and I hope it serves you well and draws you nearer to your angelic guides. But most of all, I hope it puts a smile on your face.

While connecting with the archangels is a perfect way to establish and maintain a life-nurturing relationship with the Spirit—the essence of God that flows through us all—I have come to find, through my decade of experience with those seeking angelic guidance, that too many of us simply cannot fathom what it's like to be in the company of angels. We want these divine creatures by our side, but we believe we are unworthy of their attention. I've come to believe that this sense of insecurity and low self-worth stems from our lack of understanding of angels and the Divine in general. Many of us are conditioned to think a certain way about angels and the realm of the Spirit, and for the most part, that's fine. This book is not about debunking traditional or ancient texts on these divine creatures, but rather about adding to what we already know.

As humanity changes, so does the universe around it (or vice versa), and that includes our angelic friends. In order to communicate and interact with us, the angels must change as we change—or everything will be lost in translation between God and man. I think humanity has suffered gravely from centuries of misinterpretation as it is. Isn't it about time we all got on the same page with those who actually *know* how the universe works? By "those," I mean the archangels, the ones actually designated by the Creator to serve as our teachers and guides.

What you are going to find in the upcoming pages is based on my personal relationship with archangels and spirit teachers, along with some old-fashioned research. I hope the information inspires and uplifts your spirit, but most of all, I hope it encourages you to establish and maintain a direct connection with your spiritual teachers so that you can discover the awe and enchantment that is your life's path.

Connecting with the Divine is not about rites and rituals; it's simply about cherishing the fact that you are a child of the Creator. It's about love and learning, about joy and compassion, about imagination and creativity. The angels, Heaven's messengers and conductors of the cosmos, aren't floating above you and passing judgment; they are beside you, lovingly guiding your every step. They are your companions in spirit—your brothers and sisters, helping you to navigate life and get the most spiritual growth you can out of every life experience.

MY ROAD TO MEDIUMSHIP

People have called me a psychic or a medium (or even a nutcase), but I'm honestly not hung up on titles. However, I am moved to remind these same people that all human beings have a connection to "the other side," albeit on different levels. The ability to "connect" is no more or less intriguing a skill than is singing, painting, or martial arts. Generally speaking, every person is capable of making this connection to the other side, and should not feel that such a skill (or gift, or talent) is only for the select few. Your innate gifts only require nurturing, practice, and dedication to make them blossom.

Primarily, I consider myself a telephone operator to the angels—in that I connect you with the guardian angels and spirit guides who are already with you, all the time. My job is not fortune-telling. I do not have the winning lottery numbers, nor am I going to tell you whether or not your boyfriend is cheating on you. My purpose is to serve as a guide, helping you connect with your angels every day. By opening up and allowing them to work in your life, you will find new paths for facilitating healing, gaining wisdom, and increasing self-awareness.

My road to mediumship with the angels was a rocky one paved with my own rebellion, resistance, and old-fashioned stubbornness. Though I was raised with a solid Christian foundation—Lutheran and Pentecostal—angels were never a part of my family's paradigm. As a child, I was deeply religious; perhaps more so than my parents, for I was the one to drag everyone out of bed on Sundays for church and the first one to cry if we were snowed in or my parents just didn't feel like going. My religious upbringing didn't prepare me very well for what I was to encounter as I got older, however. If anything, it just opened up a whole new panoply of questions that wouldn't get answered until I was well into my adult years.

While my first contact with my spirit guide, Jake, occurred when I was an adult, it wasn't my first experience with (what I then considered) the Unknown. My first childhood memory of a paranormal encounter happened on Thanksgiving Day when I was only eight. My mom was up before dawn that day, preparing the turkey for a long, lazy bake in the oven. And I was up right along with her, helping her cook (mostly by tasting everything she prepared) and darting in and out of the family room to catch a glimpse of the parades on television. I'm sure I was a whir to my mother, who worked tirelessly over the stove all morning and well into the afternoon, but I obviously wasn't too quick to notice a sparkle of light—which seemed to hover above a chair at the dining room table like a tiny fairy. I dismissed it as sunlight reflecting off the chandelier's crystals, but as the sun made its way around the house and the shadows of early evening approached, the light continued to pulsate slowly, even as my family sat at the table enjoying dinner. If I glanced at the spot where it hovered, it would disappear. If I looked away, it would reappear. After a while I thought maybe my eyeglasses needed adjusting.

Later that evening, my parents sat on the couch like two over-stuffed bears ready for hibernation and we children began the ritual of putting up the Christmas tree. And it was then—somewhere between sorting the branches of the artificial tree limbs and piecing together the snow pump that sprayed fake snow—that I saw Mrs. Moore sitting at the dining room table. Out of the corner of my eye, I saw her guffaw at us kids as we bumbled along. I snapped my gaze around; she was sitting where the orb of light had been earlier. I blinked, and she smiled and waved. I blinked again, and she was gone.

Who was Mrs. Moore? My favorite Lunch Lady at school. She had passed away suddenly at the beginning of the year.

My next childhood experience happened on a wintry January morning in 1986, when I was twelve years old. I was in bed catching a last few minutes of sleep before rising for school, and dreaming I was watching the news on television. A space shuttle had just been launched, but the anchorman became hysterical and began reporting that the shuttle had exploded. I was a bit shaken when I awoke, but I quickly dismissed the dream—not only did I not have plans to be on a space shuttle anytime soon, but I was hardly interested in the U.S. space program at the time.

Later that day, an announcement came over the school's PA system that the space shuttle Challenger had exploded just seconds after launch. At the time, I didn't put two and two together. In fact, I remember thinking, *what exploded?* I'd had no prior knowledge that a shuttle was being launched. The only thing on my mind at the time was what mom might have been cooking for dinner and if my favorite rerun of *The Jeffersons* was coming on.

Well, to my dismay, there was no rerun of *The Jeffersons* when I got home. Instead, I found myself staring at the continuous replays of the Challenger tragedy on television. A few hours passed before I remembered the dream—and when I did, a chill moved through me. I tried telling my mother about the dream, but her reply did little to allay my fears.

"Sometimes it just happens," Mom said. "You'll see things before they come to pass. I get that all the time." She was basically dismissing the premonition as easily as she dismissed the tooth fairy. Still, having dreamt of something so tragic and then seeing it come true, I found myself afraid to sleep, afraid to dream. I didn't sleep much for a few months.

It was during these waking hours in the middle of the night, however, that even stranger things began to happen. My first encounter with a haunting happened late one evening as I wandered the house while my parents slept. While pacing the upstairs corridor, I glanced toward the staircase banister to see a little girl about my age peering back at me, her hands wrapped around the ornate, wrought-iron bars. She tilted her head and regarded me a moment. I froze in my steps, staring wide-eyed at her because she was on the opposite side of the topmost banister, the side where there were no steps for her to stand on. So, like any frightened kid, I screamed for my dad, who ran into the hallway and turned on the light. The apparition disappeared.

Many years passed before my father shared with me that a little girl and her mother had died in a house fire just a year before we moved in. Though this revelation gave me little relief, it did at least explain why I hated my bedroom closet so much. Yes, I was afraid of the closet monster like any other kid, but now I knew that what I was detecting from my closet was the fear of that little girl who perished of smoke inhalation inside it.

But the little girl on the staircase was not the only ghost to get my attention during my twenty-year stay in that house. There was another ghost who walked the hallways, too, but only on autumn evenings. He was tall and broad-shouldered like my father. It took a few sightings, out of the corner of my eye, before I realized that it was not my father walking past my bedroom, but a mysterious man in overalls. He would walk into my parents' room and disappear. I found this out the hard way one evening when I got up to follow him, only to enter the empty room, get spooked, and go downstairs—to see my dad fast asleep on the couch.

Given that I was a child known for an overactive imagination, my parents never really did understand the level of fear I endured many nights in our family home. But finally, as I got older, a woman in white came to my rescue. I often saw her at the door of my bedroom, peeking in with a soft smile. After the initial shock of her presence, I came to be comforted by her as long as I could see her straight-on. When she appeared in mirrors, though, that would scare the bejesus out of me every time. But with her around, I never saw the ghost in overalls again. Was she protecting me? Did she oust the autumn-walker? I will probably never know. All I do know is that upon her arrival, he disappeared, and I was grateful.

So no, I was not the happiest kid in Detroit at the time. I had a retired father whose main concern was how big of a fish he'd catch at Belle Isle and a mother who just wanted to go to work to get away from my father. So, alone and without very much knowledge, I faced my fears, ghosts, premonitions, and déjà vu moments until my teenage years, where all the things that used to frighten me suddenly became … cool.

Oddly, all the paranormal things that happened to me as a child ceased to happen in my teenage years. I'm not sure if it was because I was trying too hard, or simply because I was trying to entertain my high school friends. Appropriately enough, since I grew up during the height of the heavy metal 1980s, any rock group that claimed to reveal secrets of the Unknown in their album lyrics or covers—anyone whose music (when played backwards) was some ancient incantation opening a portal to some unknown universe—ranked very high on my wish list at birthdays and Christmas. And so it was with all of my friends; we lived in a world of dark fantasy. Of course, having older (and hence oblivious) parents was an advantage. Unlike my friends' parents, mine had no idea what I was into and never questioned it (to my great relief, since there was not a single Iron Maiden or Ozzy Osbourne album I didn't own).

The creepy, spooky, and dangerous had now become fun, hip, and totally awesome. And like every other teen of that era, I bought into all the smoke and mirrors for a while; well, at least until I found out years later that Mötley Crüe knew just as much about the workings of the deepest circles of Hell as Tipper Gore. By the 1990s, however, heavy metal had become American kitsch and so had demons, devils, and witchery.

While attending college, though, I had discovered that heavy metal didn't die. It just went underground, added a smooth groove, and called itself Goth. Okay, so vampires were the "in thing" now, and I was fine with that. However, not only had I gotten cornered by resident campus blood-suckers, but I'd also been set upon by resident campus Bible-thumpers. Some might give a sigh of relief to hear that I went along with the Bible-thumpers, but I had to—they scared me more than the vampires did. In fact, they frightened me so deeply into thinking I was going to Hell that I wanted just to leave college and become a nun.

For a few years, I was feverishly enthralled with church. I was in Sunday service for three hours, sometimes six. I was at Bible study on Tuesdays and prayer meetings on Wednesdays. I preached to my niece about hanging out in night clubs, preached to my mom about smoking, and preached to my dad about not going to church anymore. I think I became a scarier person than I was when I was wearing bangle bracelets up to my elbows, Stevie Nicks gypsy skirts, and Metallica T-shirts. Basically, my family hated me, but that didn't stop me from sitting in the pew and absorbing every word coming from the pulpit. Oh, I was on a mission to Heaven, and I refused to let heathen friends and family members dissuade me.

I was a regular attendee at my church, one of the most popular churches in Detroit, long before the congregation's membership exploded and the service went from spreading the Word to a three-hour gospel concert. So I read the Bible every night, studying it until my eyes crossed, all in an attempt to get to know God for myself. I wanted to be closer to Him, enveloped by Him, but nothing was moving in my soul. It was as if I had hit a strange plateau on a diet where, no matter how hard I worked out or starved myself, I just wasn't losing weight.

Then I started to question my past and began sobbing in prayer, begging God to forgive me for all the times I'd played Ozzy backward or cranked up a raunchy Kiss tune whenever I saw an old couple pass my car. I begged Him to let me make up for all the times I fell asleep while studying the Bible or was late to church service. Lightning frightened me, and the notion of death sent a chill through my bones that no words can ever describe. I had become so terrified of Hell and God's wrath that I became a recluse, fearful of the world around me. And that's when the dreams came back—dreams I hadn't had since I was a child.

I began to have dreams of Armageddon and the Rapture, and (of course) of missing the Rapture like missing a bus in downtown Detroit in the pouring rain—I'd just grin and bear it because there was never any shelter or security around. Sleep eluded me for the second time in my life, and again my mother dismissed the dreams as a blend of a hyperactive imagination and serious guilt about causing her so much grief as a teenager. So, I had to face the Unknown on my own for a bit longer. Many times I wanted to go to my pastor, but when the pastor of your church (along with just about every other church officer) is an international gospel star, it seems you might have a better chance of getting answers from their booking agents. I turned to the Bible, but answers weren't coming quickly enough for my liking. So I got back on my knees, and, instead of begging for forgiveness, sent a barrage of questions heavenward.

I warn you now that if you decide to do this in earnest, if you start asking God questions, He will answer you. But know that He may not answer you in the way you're expecting.

One evening in 1993, as I was well into a good hour of prayer, my bedside soaked with tears, my knees numb, and my sinuses completely clogged from bowing my head and crying at the same time . . . I heard a whisper of a voice.

"Chantel, you are not being punished. There is nothing to forgive." Startled, I straightened up and looked around the bedroom, blinking away tears. And then, as if on instinct, I looked up to my ceiling.

"I don't know what You want from me, Lord. I'm afraid." I trembled and wiped at my face, waiting for that ceiling to open up and flood my bedroom with a bright beam of white light. It never did, but the voice subtly responded.

"Wisdom eradicates fear. There are many things for you to learn and accomplish in this lifetime. I will work through you, and you will teach and you will heal others. So now is a time for gathering wisdom and understanding."

I curled up again and shook my head. "No, Lord. Don't do that to me. I don't want that responsibility. I don't want to teach. I just want to live."

"You can shoulder the responsibility, Chantel."

"But I'm nobody. I'm not even all that knowledgeable with the Bible. I can't sing. I get nervous when I talk to people. I have a horrible memory …"

"You forget one important thing."

"Like I said, I have a horrible memory."

"Chantel, you are still my child."

"Lord, I listened to the rock-n-roll radio station today."

"I know, and … ?"

"I liked it. Sorry."

"You are still my child."

"I almost feel sorry for You, Lord, that You're stuck with me. Now about this job. What am I supposed to teach? And I thought You took care of the healing department."

"You will know. Read, learn. You will know."

"Lord?"

"Yes?"

"I can't picture myself talking to groups of people 'n stuff. I hate giving speeches."

"Open your eyes, Chantel. Be watchful. Be mindful."

With that, a small summer storm moved in and I fell asleep there on my knees, thinking God must be desperate if He was soliciting *me*. I guessed it was just hard for Him to find good help these days.

One might think that I embraced this revelation and spent the next ten years of my life piously following every whisper that came to me from the heavens. In actuality, I spent the next decade running like hell away from something I just didn't want to do—serve as a messenger of God, in church or otherwise. I was terrified of speaking, first and foremost, and then I also feared the responsibilities of letting heavenly hosts speak through me. Me? Little, insignificant me? I was hardly worthy! So with my fear and self-loathing, I turned away from God and religion altogether—at least for a while—and instead focused on a much more mundane life of education and work.

Still, every now and then, curiosity would pinch me and I'd find myself in the library for hours, reading about the religions and cultures of the world. After a year or so of this, I got tired of simply sitting on the sidelines and decided I wanted to explore different thoughts, philosophies, and beliefs. I wanted to get down into the trenches and talk to others who had beliefs that differed from mine. I wanted to know what fortified their faith and how they had come to the knowing that their path was *the* correct path.

I already had a background in Earth-based religions and New Age thought, having studied such pioneers such as Gerald Gardner and Edgar Cayce, but I wanted to branch out beyond the West. I began studying Eastern thought, only to literally (as well as figuratively) find refuge in Buddhism. Naturally, the study of Buddhism led me to the study of Hinduism. These philosophies stunned me. As a Christian who had never before entertained notions like nirvana or atman, I was moved in a way I had never been moved before. These philosophies simply felt *right*—and it was actually Buddhism that led me to a greater understanding of Jesus than any Christian gospel I had ever read.

Even with this revelation, however, years of religious conditioning held fast. I lived much of the decade studying by flashlight, as if to hide from God that I was veering away from the Christian path. I spent years praying, and crying and feeling guilty and praying more, only to finally arrive at my own conclusions about spirituality: we all come from one Source and to it we shall return. The term for this thought is *pantheism*. Today, I can say with great conviction that I believe in this philosophy, but when I adopted it years ago, I was not so brazen.

One might think that my resistance to mediumship with the angels was just me fighting God over "leaving" the religion of my parents, and their parents, and all those generations before me. Quite the contrary. I didn't have to leave my Christian faith. Though I embrace and respect the philosophies of many religions and those who follow them, the cornerstone of my life remains Jesus of Nazareth. I'll boastfully say that no one loves Him more, or is a bigger fan of His than I am. Perhaps unlike others in the Christian faith, I see Him *literally* as my father—He's my family, my mentor, my authority, as well as a deity to be worshipped.

My resistance to accepting my role as an angel medium, then, came simply from my refusal to believe the idea that we all come from one Source. My struggles were against Jesus, Buddha, my spirit guides, and other ascended masters—who all insisted that this idea was true. So for years, with much fear and trepidation, I questioned and tested and questioned some more until the answers started flowing in like floodwaters, sweeping me off my feet and carrying me into the realm of angelology.

Now, many who are steadfast in their religious beliefs have asked me, "Why do I need to talk to angels when I got Jesus?" Well, the answer is simple: you don't *need* to do anything. The point is, many of us suffer from what I suffered from my entire life—a serious inferiority complex that tells us we are too unworthy to go before our gods to ask for help and answers. For me, since I feel such a strong connection to Jesus, my connection to the angels is simple. If Jesus (the king of angels) is my Father, that would make the angels … my brothers and sisters. And if you have siblings, especially older siblings, you know that it is much easier to go ask them a question than it is to ask your parent. Having a sibling to talk to gives you the chance to test the waters, to see if your question will warrant a punishment of some kind. The angels have been most helpful in answering a lot of my questions, but a lot of times I have in fact gotten, "Go ask your Father." And so, with quaking knees, I approach my mentor with a bowed head and hopes that my question isn't off-limits.

I have been at this for a long while now, and (God knows) I've asked many a heavy and heady question. But I've yet to get yelled at. The universe has tenderly and lovingly guided me through all my spiritual learning: from my mother's belief in faith healing (which I later incorporated into my Usui Reiki practice), to my formal studies in metaphysics and comparative religion, to all the clients I've had the pleasure of connecting with through my lectures and consultations. And so here I am—a natural clairvoyant, clairaudient, clairsentient, and angel medium who has traveled a long, arduous spiritual road to get to a place in my life to where I can, frankly, laugh about it.

I think, when it comes to our quest for spirituality, we sometimes take ourselves too seriously. I know I did for the first thirty years of my life. I found myself stupefied as to why I hadn't spiritually matured, despite all my earnest efforts. It wasn't until Archangel Michael came into my life and said "Chantel, you really need to chill out, lighten up, and learn to laugh!" that I allowed myself to laugh—and to be grateful for each moment I spend with the angels.

Many of us who mindfully walk a spiritual path may have forgotten how to truly enjoy life, how to laugh a little.

I pray this book will help you to remember.

Brightest Blessings,

Chantel Lysette

WHEN ANGELS WHISPER DO YOU LISTEN?

The angels first came to me when I was in my early twenties … and I met them with much skepticism and rebellion. For the longest time I thought I was losing my mind, until, of course, they began to prove themselves again and again through the accuracy of the information they provided. Although the angels have been with me for nearly two decades now, I must admit that many years passed before I became accustomed to their presence.

I sincerely pray that it does not take anyone else two decades to get to know the angels! I hope this book can serve as a bit of a shortcut, helping you get to know your angels on a personal level: their distinct personalities, likes and dislikes, skills and delegated tasks. Get to know them better, and you open yourself up to the privilege of watching them in action within your own life. While you may have a front-row seat to this game that is your life, just think of the view if you were watching it through angelic binoculars. Wow, all of a sudden it becomes so much clearer, and you can see everything with greater meaning and purpose.

In this book, I explain how to connect with your angels for guidance and companionship. The key is to go to your angels not only in times of crisis but in your daily life as well, simply because you love them and enjoy their company. The primary reason many of us have a hard time connecting with the angels is because we go to our celestial guides in a state of need—uptight, upset, anxious, desperate, and all the other wrong things. At that point, we're looking for help—a desired result—not a connection with the angels. I call this the "emergency room syndrome." When you're in serious, excruciating pain, you couldn't care less how the attending doctor's family is or how his golf swing's going. All you want is to ease the pain as quickly as *inhumanly* possible.

And so it is with many of us and our relationship with the angels. We go when the going has already gotten tough and there's little room in our minds to actually take in the awe, wonder, and beauty that is the angel. I'm not saying that Michael wants you to ask him how his archery training has been the last few centuries (though he'd love it if you did). I'm saying that if you go to your angels when you're not in a panic, it will make it easier for you to be receptive and accepting of their guidance when all heck is breaking loose. Imagine your relief if you went to the emergency room and saw that the attending doctor was a familiar and cherished family friend. Wouldn't that alone ease some of your pain? It would certainly give you relief to know that the doctor had a vested interest in your well-being, rather than just fear of a malpractice lawsuit.

Yes, the angels work well in a crisis. But why wait for a crisis when you can engage them and interact with them on a daily basis? They're already beside you with their wings and arms open. Embrace them, and be inspired and encouraged by what they can do as companions along your spiritual journey.

While you're at it, let go of the notion that you are unworthy of their time. My clients often say they aren't comfortable with the idea of casual angelic chit-chat; it feels like they're bothering the angels with a whole bunch of "nothing" when there's no "need" to ask for their attention. But the angels are not bound by time (or anything else for that matter). They are the masters of multitasking—I've witness this firsthand while hosting my Angel Galleries (where I offer mini angel consultations in front of a live audience). If there are four participants who all have Michael as their guardian angel, it does not mean that Sue gets Michael on Monday, Lisa gets him on Tuesday, and so on. When those four participants leave the venue, Michael leaves with each one of them. He becomes *four* Michaels!

The angels can watch over you, talk with you, count the hairs on your head, count the blades of grass on your lawn, and do the same for your neighbor, your spouse, and your best friend—and never miss a beat! The angels are limitless. Interact with them, and discover for yourself how this connection can elevate your life condition and facilitate change deep within you, creating an environment of love, peace, comfort, and hope for yourself and your loved ones.

> *It is not because angels are holier than men*
> *or devils that makes them angels, but because*
> *they do not expect holiness from one another,*
> *but from God only.*
>
> —WILLIAM BLAKE

CUTTING THROUGH THE HYPE

Before we start talking about what angels are and where they come from, let's start off by laying to rest a few misconceptions about Heaven's messengers.

Angels are not short-order cooks.

Do they come when you ask? Yes. Do they *do* what you ask? Well, it all depends on if your request is in line with the Divine Order of the Universe. Many of you may know this as "God's Plan." (We'll discuss this later.)

Angels are not matchmakers.

Focus on your own spiritual growth before looking for a diversion in a mate.

Angels are not leprechauns or genies.

While you will always have exactly what you need when you need it, don't count on winning that million-dollar lottery unless it's a part of your life script. Contrary to what you may believe, winning a million dollars won't solve all your problems, so stop praying for it. If it's meant to happen, it will, whether you light ten votives at church this Sunday or stand at the corner store rubbing your "lucky" rabbit's foot.

Angels are your companions, here to help you learn and grow. They are not here to fulfill wishes. This is why some prayers are seemingly answered while others are not. It's not a matter of who God listens to; rather, it's a matter of what your life script is. The angels are your guides, your helpers along your life's journey. They are not brokers, job placement officers, or divorce lawyers. They are here only to do one thing—to guide you as you fulfill your life's purpose.

And what is that purpose? Well, that's something that you and your guides will eventually discuss. But in the meantime, know that the angels are not here to build your faith in them ... or even in God. They are here to help you build faith in yourself and to help you realize that you are a spiritual being—a vessel of God's light. As the French Jesuit scientist Teilhard

de Chardin said so eloquently, "We are not human beings on a spiritual journey. We are spiritual beings on a human journey."

THE SCRIPTED LIFE

With the growing popularity of the notion that we can have anything we want when we want it, people are spending more time on wishing and less time on spiritual growth. I must say that I find this "Universe as a Smorgasbord" concept alarmingly shortsighted. I believe we *do* have a set script in life—we *do* have a set purpose. While we are granted some leniency on the details of how we achieve our purpose, once we jump into this existence, we are locked in for the ride.

Of course, the belief of being "locked in for the ride" can be highly uncomfortable, primarily because so many people are so discontent with their lives. The notion may even sound cruel, especially to people who have experienced harsh circumstances (home displacement, poverty, loss of a parent or child—all of which I have gone through). But here's the deal, as I see it: if you focus on what you *do* have instead of what you don't have, I think you'll find something to be grateful for.

And if you are going through a major life challenge right now, please do not be disheartened. You actually have home-court advantage, in that you have the chance to find your gift now, instead of having to sift through the rubble of resentment and regret to try to find the positive later on. Heaven is in control, so let go. We go through what we go through to learn and fulfill life's destiny. Does steel bemoan the fire when it's being tempered into a sword? Does clay resent the hands of the potter or the heat of the kiln before becoming a masterpiece? This is why it's so crucial to get to know your angels on such a deep and personal level, since they can help you understand why you must go through what you must go through. No, you won't always like their answers—but you can at least find comfort in knowing that they will never leave you, not for a second, while you endure.

So what about free will? To quote Archangel Gabriel, "What about it?" From what I've seen, it doesn't exist. If you believe in God or any type of creative force or intelligent designer, the notion of free will cannot fit into the same construct. The majority of those who believe in a Creator believe that this force is either omnipotent or omnipresent, or both. Logically, then, we cannot have free will if God knows what we are going to do *before* we even do it. Given this, how can there be any such thing as "choice"? Of course, we are presented with choices all the time, but they are there as tools for learning, not as God's way of giving us freedom so that we may be judged for these decisions later.

Keep in mind that there is no "should have" in life. There is only "what is." You can't make a *wrong* choice, per se, because you are exactly where you're supposed to be when you're supposed to be. While the idea of a lack of free will seems harsh, remember that you didn't just get assigned a life and then plunked into this cold, cruel world. No, not in the least.

You, with God as your co-author, scripted your life.

God dwells within you, and you dwell within God. And while you were in the realm of the Spirit with God, you decided to dip your toes into this pool. At that point, you were in perfect knowing of the things you wanted to accomplish this lifetime. So now here you are, with the rest of us, experiencing all there is to be experienced this time around. There's nothing wrong with this system, of course, other than the fact that many of us forget our spiritual identities once we leave the realm of the Spirit. Minor detail, right? But don't fret—you can get remnants of that identity back, which will help you navigate this life a bit better.

Again, that's where the angels can help you! Of course, they help when you're in a fix, but they also help you to discover your purpose and your identity. The angels are pretty handy creatures; we humans better take advantage of their knowledge and skills.

Still, some of you may think that even if we do co-author our lives with the Divine, the notion of not having free will is frustrating. I initially thought this was a downer, too, but as I let it sink in, I realized that the greatest feeling of freedom came in understanding that God is in control of this film production called *Life*, and we are each blessed to have a role. Don't begrudge your role if you are "Night Watchman #2." Live that role as if you're going for an Oscar. After all, there is a huge audience watching in the realm of the Spirit, and they are rooting for you. They should, after all. They, like the angels, are your family. The life force, the energy that gives angels flight is the same energy at the core of every human being—the soul, the Presence of Spirit, the Presence of God.

From the Spirit above, humanity below, and all in between, we are family. Like cogs in a machine, we are all connected and we all have a place in this vast, immeasurable universe.

ARCHANGELS, OUR COMPANIONS IN SPIRIT

The word *angel* derives from the Greek word *angelos*, which literally means "messenger." The twelve angels mentioned in this book are known as archangels: "chief angels" who are delegated the task of interacting with humans. I got to know them through a process I call "reverse angel-neering." Basically, an archangel will make me aware of his presence, and then I research historical and contemporary texts to familiarize myself with him. It's how I validate an angel's presence (as well as make sure I have not yet gone insane with voices in my head—a girl can never be too sure these days).

Depending on the religious source, the actual number of archangels in Heaven varies. In the Book of Revelations, seven archangels stand before the throne of God; the Koran only mentions four, and only two by name—Michael and Djibril (Gabriel). As I mentioned earlier, the task assigned to archangels is to serve as the go-betweens for humanity and God. According to most texts, they are the only angels who deal directly with humans and their affairs.

There are many ways you can interact with these messengers. Through the skill or gift of clairaudience (clear hearing), clairsentience (clear feeling), clairvoyance (clear seeing), and claircognizance (clear knowing), as well as through dreams or just hyper-awareness of the physical world around you, you can connect and create a beautiful, life-long relationship with your angels, one that is full of awe and profound growth.

But Chantel, what if I don't have any of these gifts? you may ask. Ah, but you do! We all do! These skills, singularly and more commonly referred to as "the sixth sense," are as common as the *other* five senses. As you ask your angels to come into your life, you will become aware of which skill you are best at. Some people are better at hearing than seeing, while others are better at feeling, or knowing. Some people are good with all of the above; the point is that no one is completely bereft of the sixth sense. So, while working to establish contact with the angels, focus your awareness on the world around you (as I did) by looking for signs and symbols—tangibles.

This is what I've called "hyper-awareness." Other people may call this "coincidence," but don't sell yourself short by trivializing your experiences. We live in such a distracted society that the majority of us walk through life completely oblivious to what's going on around us. But through hyper-awareness of your immediate world, you can create a better interaction with your angels. The angels send signs of their presence all the time, although too few of us see them. These signs of validation are the angels' way of calibrating you for bigger and better things; ergo, the development of your sixth sense. If you ask Raphael for a sign and he whispers, "Look for a dove," it doesn't mean that you go out on your front porch and stare at the sky all day. Staring at the sky would cause you to miss the convoy of Dove Ice Cream trucks that roll by your house—due to a road construction detour, no doubt.

So, why didn't Raphael say, "Look for a convoy of Dove Ice Cream trucks"? Well, he might just say that to some of you, but for many of us who are hard of hearing, the keyword "dove" will suffice. As you grow in your communication/sixth sense skills, it may seem that the angels become a lot more specific. I've been working with them for nearly two decades, and they still tend to work within the obscure and abstract when it comes to my personal life. But during consultations for my clients, the angels can be very specific. Each person is different—the angels know even better than we do what languages we're most fluent in, and will speak to us in ways we can understand. Yet remember that all the while, they're trying to elevate your consciousness by teaching you their language: the language of the Spirit, the language of the universe.

ESTABLISHING CONNECTIONS

The first step to connecting with the angels is simply having the willingness to do so. You must approach the connection as a child might approach the first day of school, with openness and an eagerness to learn. Of course, adults often approach life with a tight grip on what they already think they know, and are not often willing to unlearn all that they have learned thus far (this tendency is evident in the snail-pace evolution of schools of religion and philosophy).

Human beings are so attached to tradition and the status quo that their thoughts and beliefs can quickly become outmoded, inapplicable to the inevitable changes occurring around them. After all, the Creator and Creation are in constant flux, ever changing. You do not need philosophy books or scientific data to convince you of this, for the evidence of growth, change, evolution (or whatever you wish to call it) beckons to be noticed every day. Seasons change. Weather and climates change. Even the Earth's poles are shifting; so, how dare we as humans force upon the realm of the Spirit the notion that change cannot be possible?

It is often this unwillingness to change, to seek new territory, or simply to ask questions that keeps many of us from connecting to the Divine. (I liken this to the old belief that the world was flat and that the Earth was the center of the universe.) We must approach new spiritual territory like a daring explorer on a new adventure—not with the attitude that we already know a lot, but with the attitude that we know absolutely nothing at all. This can be an unsettling endeavor for those of us who have grown up within boundaries and constructs that teach us not to question our reality. Of course, if everyone had obeyed such teachings, I wonder if civilization would have advanced as much as it has in the last thousand years.

So, let's say you decide to take the first step toward new discoveries: what next? Surrender. Is this an act of letting go, of relinquishing control? Is it a matter of taking leaps of faiths at every turn? Yes—but do not make the mistake of thinking of it as an act of weakness. If anything, it is probably the greatest act of courage you'll ever do. To surrender, you must bolster yourself up enough to face, and let go of, all your fears. You cannot say, "God, I surrender, but don't take my job, my house, my family, my car, my friends..."

Surrendering means strengthening yourself for whatever may come your way. To surrender means not being attached to desired outcomes. Surrendering is your way of saying, "All

34

right, Heaven. I'm serious about my spiritual learning. Let's do this." As you say this, gazing skyward, you may quake in uncertainty. Your voice may even crack a little. But in the act of surrendering, you have just taken your first step toward getting to know the Divine, as well as discovering your place within its grand scheme. To guide you along the way, of course, are your angels—and they are very patient, loving, and willing teachers.

ANGELS AND THE SIXTH SENSE

While all angels and spirit teachers will communicate with you in the way that you will best understand, I have discovered that the archangels also rule over certain modalities of the sixth sense. Of course, while they may rule a certain area, their communication is not limited to that one modality. "Ruling" a modality simply means that those of us who discover a budding skill or gift can attribute this discovery to the help and guidance of its governing angel. For example, if you realize that images you're seeing in your mind's eye (clairvoyance) are manifesting in the physical world, you can thank Archangel Uriel. Also, Uriel would be your guardian angel during this time, helping you grow and flourish as you hone your gift.

Below you will find a list of intuitive gifts (collectively know as the sixth sense) and the angels who govern them. In the field of parapsychology—the study of phenomena that cannot be explained by natural law—the sixth sense is formally referred to as ESP (extrasensory perception).

Clairaudience (clair = clear; audience = hearing)

DEFINITION: The power or faculty of hearing something not present to the ear but regarded as having objective reality. (*Webster's Third New International Dictionary*)

RULING ANGEL: Gabriel. Gabriel loves to talk; after all, he is the angel of communication. You will often hear his words of wisdom whispered in your right ear.

Clairsentience (sentience = feeling)

DEFINITION: The ability to feel or sense something not physically accessible by the five senses. (*Webster's*)

RULING ANGEL: Michael. In his abundant, radiant energy, Michael often sends heat flashes to those he works with. (Not hot flashes, ladies.)

Clairvoyance (voyance = seeing)

DEFINITION: 1: The power or faculty of discerning objects not present to the senses; 2: Ability to perceive matters beyond the range of ordinary perception. (*Webster's*)

RULING ANGEL: Uriel. Uriel is a stickler for making sure his messages are clearly understood, and will therefore send

physical images to reinforce the mental images you receive from him.

Claircognizance (cognizance = knowing)

DEFINITION: The ability to suddenly know information without prior reference or knowledge of how the information was acquired. (*Webster's*)

RULING ANGEL: Raphael. Raphael is the angel of wisdom, and will whisper messages and ideas so subtly that you'll think you thought of them yourself.

Given these definitions, your next question is most likely, *Chantel, how do I know the difference between my imagination, my inner voice, and the voice of an angel?*

Here is what I would suggest: think of your imagination as a bridge to your inner voice, your intuition. By letting go of preconceived notions and entertaining the miraculous possibilities that can result from connecting with your spirit teachers, you are putting yourself in a place of surrender, a place where your mind and soul are open to experiencing what you may have at one point thought was impossible. By allowing your imagination to flow, you are engaged in the creative processes of the universe. You are moving yourself ever closer to direct alignment with the Creator, because you are moving away from the obstacles of conditioned thoughts and expectations.

Your imagination is the key to establishing and maintaining a fruitful relationship with your spirit teachers. In other words, through honing your creative skill and creative energy, you can tap into your intuitive energies. You can achieve this through meditation, active visualization, yoga, or dream journals (Raphael and Cassiel love weaving in and out of dreams). Experiment a little until you find a method that best works for you.

Always remember that you are made of the same beautiful light that flows out from God, through the angels and all the benevolent hosts of Heaven. And where there is light, no darkness can dwell. I feel the need to say that for those of you who may still be a bit apprehensive about making spiritual connections.

In Matthew 12:22–28, Jesus healed a man who was blind, mute, and said to be possessed by the devil. When the Pharisees, the ancient authorities of the Jewish faith, got wind of Jesus' actions, they accused him of being in league with the demon Beelzebub. Jesus responded with a logical argument: since "every city or house divided against itself shall not stand," then "if Satan cast out Satan, he is divided against himself; how shall then his kingdom stand?" Jesus went on to say, "if I cast out devils by the Spirit of God, then the kingdom of God is come unto you." And so the kingdom of God has come upon us all. If one works within the realm of Light and lives within the realm of Light, there's no need to fear evil forces; the only thing to be concerned about is yourself. (Michael once said to me, "Chantel, I can protect you from all but one thing in this universe: yourself. You are *so* on your own with that.")

If all else fails and you're not seeing progress in your communication/sixth sense skills, be patient and rely on hyperawareness. The angels know best, and will always guide you in a way that is most beneficial to you. After all, you may think you're ready for something, but your angels know if you truly are or not. And while you're asking them for help with your gift, also ask for help with your patience. Keep in mind that it's taken me nearly two decades to get to this point—and I'm still learning something new every day.

Final Tips on Communication

Establishing connections with the angels doesn't have to be a long, ritualized process. Some of my clients begin by simply asking for the angels to speak to them. Other clients tend to struggle along, turning the experience into some strange ten-step program that only leaves them exasperated. There is no formula ensuring that your connection with the angels will happen within a set time frame, but hopefully the pointers below will help smooth the process and make your learning experience an enjoyable one.

Take the word "coincidence" out of your vocabulary. Nothing happens by accident. Nothing.

Surrender and let go of fear. Know that everything that happens to you is all a part of what Archangel Michael calls "God's great equation." You are and always will be exactly where you're supposed to be when you're supposed to be there.

Be patient. Let communication with the angels happen organically. Don't try to force it. Just know that even if you can't hear or see your angels, it doesn't mean they're not there. For some people, the angelic connection can happen overnight, but don't be upset if it doesn't. The angels aren't ignoring you; there just are other things in your life that you need to work on first. The angels will always give you signs as to what those things are.

Show gratitude! For every blessing big and small, be grateful. And for every challenge and obstacle, be grateful. Be grateful for hard times, too. Those are periods where you experience your greatest growth.

Remove judgment. There is no such thing as "good" or "bad." The notions of good and bad are subjective and linked to how you *feel* about a situation, not to what spiritually propels you forward. Know that your spiritual growth is the angels' main objective. In that, they are driven by your purpose, not by what makes you happy (or sad).

Understand that there is a potential for frustration. The angels are here to help you grow. Period. There will be days when you wish you never saw an angel, because you can't always see far enough down the road to comprehend why you lost your job, car, and significant other all in one week. But as Michael once told me, "Chantel, don't be afraid. You can't see the finish line of this race, but I can. And I know you are going to finish gloriously." I would usually mumble something sarcastic back at him, but he would only chuckle because, after all, he is telling the truth even if I don't want to believe it. And so it is with you. The angels expect frustration, and perhaps even a few choice words thrown their way. They can take it, and all they'll throw back is unyielding love and patience.

FREQUENTLY ASKED QUESTIONS
ABOUT ANGELS

I've discovered, during the question-and-answer segment of my Angel Galleries, that audiences are more interested in the personal lives of the angels than anything else. Following their lead, I've asked and answered a series of FAQs, below, drawn from a decade of discussing angels with clients, audiences, and friends and family alike. I hope this section addresses any general curiosities you have about the angels. After all, the more you know about them, the more comfortable you'll feel about them—and the easier it will be to connect with them.

WHAT DO ANGELS LOOK LIKE?

The Western image of an angel is often that of a human figure dressed in white robes or medieval battle armor—and adorned with feathered wings, halos, swords, trumpets, or harps. These icons, which have been handed down to us through the centuries, have their roots in ancient Babylon and later found their way into early Judaism, Christianity, and Islam. As Gustav Davidson has pointed out, the white robes symbolize light, holiness, and purity; the wings and halos (also common in ancient Egyptian iconography) are symbols of divinity; the musical instruments are symbols of the angels' unyielding praise of God; and the swords and (later) battle armor are representations of cosmic and spiritual warfare, as well as God's wrath manifest.

From what I've experienced with the angels, I find them magnificently beautiful. And because beauty can take on many faces, so do the angels. They come to us in ways we are comfortable with. They are of no particular race, color, or culture. There's no favored eye color or hair color. They can be male or female. Gabriel first came to me as "Gabrielle," and then changed his tune about twelve hours later because I wasn't comfortable with a female authority in my life (I had lost both my mother and my adopted mother-in-spirit to cancer just months prior to his arrival).

While I have seen some of the archangels flash their wings, I've not seen them don halos. This is not to say they do not have a luminescence about them. They are beings of light, and that light radiates from the entire body, in all directions. As for harps, well, I've yet to see an angel with a harp; even Sandalphon, patron of music, seems to leave the stringed instrument at home, bringing with him instead boxed gifts, a garland of flowers, or candy. (He sounds like the perfect gentleman, doesn't he?) As for some of the other angels, Michael and Uriel keep their swords handy; Gabriel totes a tome or his trumpet; and Raphael walks with a staff.

When the angels aren't taking on human forms, they are formless bodies of gold and white light. Imagine luminous, golden, jellyfish-like creatures against a sea of black, with thin tendrils and wisps of white light flowing in all directions. With each graceful move of a wisp or tendril, tiny specs of gold and white dust are shed, creating delicate comet tails. Each particle of light that sheds away from an angel's greater body—their source—has the potential to create another identical angel with full knowledge and capabilities. Remember what I mentioned earlier, about Michael becoming multiple Michaels when he leaves with the audience members of Angel Galleries? We're not talking about clones here, where each generation becomes weaker the further you move down the line; angels are limitless—and if Michael has to split off into six billion Michaels to watch over every person on this planet, he can, without losing a single trace of power. Now that's *serious* energy we're working with, folks.

Angels can take many forms, choosing whatever form they must to get a job done. That's why you hear that old saying, something to the effect of "be careful how you treat a beggar on the streets; he just might be an angel testing your charity."

While the beggar himself might not be an angel, celestial forces did move him to put out his empty hand to you, not to the other two people passing by. The angels are constantly working and watching.

Could my pet Fluffy be an angel? Wrapped in fur instead of linen? I don't see why not. Cassiel has taken on the form of dragons, while Uriel has taken on the form of a phoenix. Anything is possible. The point is to remember that the angels interact with us both directly and indirectly. Fluffy may not be Raphael, but could very well have been a gift from Raphael to serve as a loyal and protective companion.

> *The angels taken collectively are called heaven,*
> *for they constitute heaven; and yet that which makes*
> *heaven in general and in particular is the Divine*
> *that goes forth from the Lord and flows into the angels*
> *and is received by them.*
>
> —EMANUEL SWEDENBORG

WHAT DO ANGELS SOUND LIKE?

This all depends on who's doing the listening. Some people may hear whispers in their right ear. Others may have a thought they think is their own. Again, angels connect with us in ways we're comfortable with. If you had a high school teacher with a shrill voice, which still makes your skin crawl when you think of her twenty years later, surely the angels are not going to communicate with you in that voice. There's also a high probability they're not going to spring Shakespearian lines on you or come off sounding like Charlton Heston in *The Ten Commandments*—unless that's what you want to hear. The angels speak in ways we are receptive to, but I'll have to admit that of all the archangels I've worked with, Archangel Michael seems to have the best handle on contemporary American vernacular and slang. With him, "it's all good" (literally).

But let's keep things simple. If you are testing your clairaudience frequencies, go with what is the most soothing and calming. Going for Hollywoodized versions of biblical figures won't help you. That's putting your guides in an authoritarian position and saying to yourself, "I'm not worthy." You are a child of God, so of course you're worthy. Talk to the angels like they're beloved family, not priests or royalty, and you'll get responses in the same way.

If you're unsure about your clairaudience skills, don't worry. The angels know how to get their points across, whether through music, movies, television, books, etc. In today's age, they have more ways than ever to get their messages through. If you're a gentleman who just had a first date with the woman of your dreams and you ask Michael for his thoughts on the situation, don't ignore the fact that you heard the song "Devil in a Blue Dress" three times while sitting in rush-hour traffic the next morning, especially if your date had on one of those cute, form-fitting sundresses in blue (with butterfly clips in her hair and a cute pair of matching flip-flops). Now, while some men wouldn't mind a "hot" date like that, just know that Michael did his best to warn you that you're going to get burned. Of course, he already knows what choice you're going to make, but tosses the warnings out there anyhow as a way of calibrating you for the next time you decide to turn into a Tex Avery cartoon character.

Same goes for you, ladies. Did you just have a great date last night? Did he seem too good to be true? Did you hear "Maniac" on the radio twice and see it on VH1 Classic before going to bed? Take a hint! It may not refer to the gentleman directly, but to his insane ex-girlfriend who will keep calling your cell phone and hanging up.

All in all, the angels will choose the avenues of communication that you will be most receptive to. The key is listening, and listening often to messages we might not want to hear. Given this, one of the most important parts of connecting with your angel guides is being honest with yourself and understanding that whatever they tell you is truly in your best interest, even if it stings your pride, your ego, or your sense of security.

I liken some communication with the angels to immunizations shots. As children, most of us are deathly afraid of the needle. All we can think of is the pain. We scream, we holler, and we clamor for mommy when that shot is coming toward us, but it will save us from life-threatening illnesses down the road. As children, we can be told that, but do we care? Heck no! All we know is that there is a needle, and right now we are experiencing pain! Who cares about "later down the road"? Our angels, that's who.

You may very well see a storm coming your way and your angel will *not* tell you that "all will be well." On several occasions, Michael has told me, "Hey, kid. This will be a tough one, but you'll get through it. I'm walking with you every step of the way." And yes, I'll scream and holler and clamor for my angels in apprehension of what is coming my way, only to look back at the experience and be grateful for the gifts it brought me. In the now, all I can see is inconvenience, pain, even loss. But in the long run, those challenges give way to greater gains. Effective communication with the angels means letting go of fear, and, as I said earlier, letting go of fear means to surrender and know that the angels are on the job. They will take care of you and support you in your spiritual growth. It is their vow to humankind. It's their vow to you.

> *Make friends with the angels, who though invisible are*
> *always with you. Often invoke them, constantly praise*
> *them, and make good use of their help and assistance*
> *in all your temporal and spiritual affairs.*
> —Saint Francis de Sales

WHERE DO ANGELS COME FROM?

From the sacred tomes of Egypt and Babylon to the poetry of Zoroaster, from the words of Abraham and Moses to the musings of Plato, from the heart of Jesus to the teachings of Muhammad, the angels have been royal ambassadors of Heaven (ancient rock stars, if you will) that have fascinated and awed us from time immemorial. The archangels we are so familiar with today come to us across a sea of time spanning beyond the reaches of written history. They've endured the ages, crossing all cultures, all religions, and all boundaries.

THE WORD "ANGEL"

Language	Word	Translation
English	*angel*	messenger
Greek	*angelos*	messenger
Hebrew	*mal'akh*	shadow side of God
Latin	*angelus*	messenger
Sanskrit	*angiras*	divine spirit
Persian	*angaros*	courier

Compiled from *A Dictionary of Angels* by Gustav Davidson

Celestial beings who serve as go-betweens for God and humankind can be found in just about every religion in the world. In Christianity, of course, they are called angels. In Judaism they are called *mal'akh*. In Islamic texts they are called *Mala'ika*. Buddhists call them *bodhisattvas*, and Hindus call them *devas*. Historically speaking, the concept of angels has been around as long as humans have contemplated what lies beyond this reality, beyond this flesh and blood, beyond the stars in the skies—the notion of Spirit.

In the Bible, there are indications that angels predate Creation itself. In the Genesis story, of course, God states, "Let us make man in our image, after our likeness" (1:26). In Psalms 8:4–5, God is asked why he is so mindful of man, "for thou hast made him a little lower than the angels." And, of course, we are given insight into their presence through the story handed down from Judaism about the Great War in Heaven—in which the most powerful angel, Lucifer, incensed by the creation of man, leads an uprising against God, only to lose to the skill and brawn of Archangel Michael. According to the story, Michael and the other archangels oust the rebels involved in the coup d'état, and one-third of Heaven's residents are cast down into Hell. Sometimes when I think of this story, I take on a very Uriel-esque attitude toward Creation: All that and you *still* made man? *Oy*!

Regardless of the religion you follow, chances are that angels or angel-type beings will be involved in the Creation tale, since one of the most common religious schematics locates humans on Earth, God in Heaven, and the angels in between. And, if you are so inclined to believe, bad angels who dwell below it all, roasting the souls of evil humans on spits with a touch of garlic, rosemary, and dash of sherry. Mmm, yummy.

The most common Western concept of angels, as we know it today, came to us in AD 325 by way of the Roman emperor Constantine, who sought to create a single, unifying religion in the Roman Empire. The new religion of Christianity, sanctioned by the state, struggled against the empire's traditional pagan roots. But the belief in *One True God* was finally established, and the demigods of paganism were replaced by what we call angels. (The same can be said of ancient Egypt, where demigods were demoted and promoted based on the ruling Pharaoh's desires at the time.) The common assumption that angels have wings may have its roots in pagan Roman lore, and may be attributable to the Roman god Mercury. As the messenger god, Mercury was depicted with wings on his feet—which today allows him to serve as the celestial version of an FTD florist.

Fast forwarding to the thirteenth century brings us to Catholic theologian and philosopher St. Thomas Aquinas, who was given visions of Heaven. Based on these visions, he offered a blueprint of the celestial realms in one of his most popular works, *Summa Theologica*. In his treatise on angels, he described a celestial hierarchy related to the angels' proximity to God:

1. Seraphim
2. Cherubim
3. Thrones
4. Dominions
5. Virtues
6. Powers
7. Principalities
8. Archangels
9. Angels

From *A Dictionary of Angels* by Gustav Davidson

He further divided these nine groups into three *choirs*, with the Seraphim, Cherubim, and Thrones making up the Angels of Contemplation choir; the Dominions, Virtues, and Powers making up the Angels of the Cosmos choir; and the Principalities, Archangels, and Angels making up the Angels of the Earth choir.

While Aquinas' work is one of the most accepted works on the hierarchy of angels, there is still a large debate about the size of the angel population. No one knows really just how many angels there are. Some theologians guesstimate thousands, and others believe that the number of angels is infinite. In my study, I've chosen to focus on twelve archangels who can be found in Judeo-Christian texts. I could go on forever listing angels, but the catch is that I only write about what I know—and the angels listed in this book are either those I have encountered within my own life or ones I've regularly consulted for clients.

All history aside, suffice it to say that angels are also children of the Creator; they came into being before the birth of humanity to be the conductors of the cosmos. They all have delegated tasks. Archangels, the focus of this book, interact directly with humanity—guiding us ever closer to understanding ourselves, and thus to an understanding of Creation and our place within it.

> *Men create gods after their own image,*
> *not only with regard to their form*
> *but with regard to their mode of life.*
> —ARISTOTLE

DO I HAVE TO BE RELIGIOUS TO HAVE THE ASSISTANCE OF ANGELS?

St. Thomas Aquinas is often credited with the following statement: *Angels transcend every religion, every philosophy, every creed. In fact, angels have no religion as we know it, as their existence precedes every religious system that has ever existed.*

As mentioned earlier, the concept of angels as we know it today has been handed down through the ages from one religion or belief to another. But let me offer up some information that may get me into a bit of hot water:

Angels, or anything in the Spirit realm, are not bound by religion per se. They don't have one. They don't follow one. And what religion you practice, or whether you practice a religion at all, doesn't matter when it comes to connecting with them. Why? Because religion is man-made. It is our way of organizing life according to what we believe pleases the Powers That Be, in order to gain blessings and promises of some reward in an afterlife. It is also our way of organizing life according to what we believe displeases the Powers That Be—in order to feel justified in separating ourselves from others and persecuting those who do not believe as we do. While in the beginning religion was about connecting to the Divine and fostering the relationship between humankind and God, it has been reduced over the centuries to serve one simple purpose: control.

Am I anti-religion? Hardly. I have a pantheistic spiritual view, believing that everything in this world comes from one Source and to that Source it all shall inevitably return. The many religions of our world have common veins, and offer great wisdom and contributions to the spiritual evolution of humankind. It's only when religion seeks to control and dictate what people should or should not believe that it oversteps its boundaries. History has shown us all too well that no good can come of such an imposition.

As I tell all my clients, it's not my job to dictate to anyone which religious path to follow. Jesus' instructions to me were quite clear when he came to me back in 1993. "You are not here to destroy nor build a belief, but to help others along the paths that they are already on." I am merely a messenger, and I must follow the example set forth by the angels: they show no preference between the religions of the world, and neither will I.

In about ninety percent of the consultations that I've done, clients voice one concern: "I just want to make sure I'm on the right path." The answer is simple. You can never stray from your right path. Your life *is* your path. This is your chosen script and you cannot veer from it. Our Creator has made sure of that. And that's one of the key tasks for the angels: to guide and instruct us as we go along, no matter where our paths may lead. To sit and ponder your choice to follow a religion, multiple religions, or no religion at all is inconsequential. You already made that choice before you were born. You already scripted it.

Whether you utter "Hail Mary," "Jesus is Lord," "Kadosh Kadosh Kadosh," "Aum Shri Ganeshaya Namah," "Om Mani Padme Om," or nothing at all, the angels are always by your side. The faith you follow does not concern them as much as the degree to which that faith contributes to your genuine spiritual growth. Genuine? Yes, because there are billions of religious people in the world. Few actualize their relationship with the Divine. A connection with God does not manifest itself through rites and rituals before an altar on holy days, but through your daily actions and deeds toward fellow human beings. Spirituality is not so much about what you believe in life, but what you do in life and how you react to life.

> *True religion is real living; living with all one's soul,*
> *with all one's goodness and righteousness.*
> —ALBERT EINSTEIN

WHAT ARE GUARDIAN ANGELS?

Traditionally speaking, guardian angels are angels that are appointed to a person at the time of birth. There is much debate about just how many guardian angels a person may have—some say you only have one, or three, or seven during a lifetime. I find this belief to be a bit restrictive; in fact, I find the whole concept of the "guardian" angel a bit misleading.

The term "guardian" implies protection from harm or misfortune. This naturally leads to the sale of many a trinket and charm embossed, engraved, or emblazed with the likeness of a particular angel—in hopes that having such a trinket will keep evil at bay. But *all* the angels of Heaven are your family. They're like your big brothers and sisters, who watch over you and help you grow and evolve into the best person you can be in this lifetime. You're not appointed one, three, or even ten angels to protect you. So, the idea of a specific "guardian" is a pretty moot

point. And just as importantly, it's is less about who is guarding us—and more about who is teaching us!

When people come up to me (usually out of the blue), often the first question they'll ask is, "Who is my guardian angel?" My usual response is, "You mean, who is your mentoring angel?" When I give angel consultations, I focus on the angel or angels I perceive in the foreground. If you have an affinity for Raphael and you come to find out that Gabriel is in the foreground, don't be dismayed! Raphael hasn't gone anywhere. It's just that Gabriel is in the foreground of your life to help mentor you in the life lessons you need to learn at this time. When those lessons are learned, Michael might step in, or Cassiel. The list of spirit teachers is endless, and the angels are always with you, watching over you. How can they not be? By default, they are connected to you by way of the Spirit of the Creator, which flows through us all.

The really neat part about mentoring angels is that they are highly consistent. As you read about their personalities in the next section, you'll discover that certain angels arrive when you're going through different stages of your life. Each angel has a specialty, and his presence in your life should not only help to quell your doubts and fears, but also should yield clues as to which areas of your life need attention and maintenance.

> *We cannot pass our guardian angel's bounds,*
> *resigned or sullen, he will hear our sighs.*
> —Saint Augustine

WHAT'S THE DIFFERENCE BETWEEN GUARDIAN [MENTORING] ANGELS, SPIRIT GUIDES & ASCENDED MASTERS?

Your guardian (I mean mentoring) angel can be your spirit guide, but not all spirit guides are angels. I usually assign the name "spirit guide" to someone who has lived in this existence and passed on, but now helps us from the Spirit realm. Many clients come to me seeking validation that their dearly departed is indeed with them, guiding them along. Our ascended friends and family members remain with us, mostly to comfort us during life's most trying challenges. They help bolster us by becoming our cheerleading section and send us messages of encouragement and faith, but do not necessarily guide us. That's a job delegated to our angels and ascended masters.

Ascended masters are those who have lived in this existence and have achieved extraordinary spiritual insight during their lifetime. Beloved spiritual masters such as Jesus, Siddhartha Gautama (the original Buddha), Mother Teresa, and Gandhi are a few examples. According to New Age thought, deities from religions worldwide are also placed in this group. I'm not against this classification, especially having worked with these types of deity energies myself. God has many faces, and, as His child, I must acknowledge them all.

We are each of us angels with only one wing,
and we can only fly by embracing one another.
—LUCRETIUS

WHY DO ANGELS ALLOW "BAD" THINGS TO HAPPEN?

If it wasn't for the idea of *good versus evil*, Hollywood would run out of material for films. According to a plethora of religious teachings, humans are eternally caught up in a crossfire of spiritual warfare between the benevolent hosts of the heavens and the diabolical demons of the infernal realms. But while the notions of good and evil have been with humankind since its beginnings, they describe one thing and one thing only: how a situation makes us feel. For example:

The harvest was bountiful this year. The gods must be pleased with the village.

Great rains came and flooded the village. We have no food. This is bad. The gods must be angry.

A great illness came to our village. Many people have died. This is bad. The demons must be cast out.

I got a pay raise and all my bills are paid. The kids are like angels and the hubby did house chores. I couldn't feel more blessed.

I lost my job and the house is in foreclosure. My husband wants a divorce and the kids want to live with him. God is punishing me. (Or the Devil is out to get me.)

When circumstances move along with our personal agenda and life flows in the direction we want it to, "life is good."

When all hell breaks loose and we're left without recourse or resources, "life is bad."

It's time to remove this limited point of view from our lives and understand what Archangel Gabriel has so eloquently expounded: "Life is." The angels do not work in terms of what makes us feel good or what makes us feel bad, but rather what serves a purpose. As discussed earlier, they are here to guide us in following our chosen script. And they're bound by the one law we're all bound by—the law of causality, or cause and effect.

Each action brings about an effect. Christians call this The Golden Rule. Buddhists call it karma. Science calls it the "butterfly effect." In essence, the angels create causes in our lives to bring about a desired effect, which in turn creates another cause in some else's life (from the trivial to the profound), and so on and so forth. There are no accidents. The ripples that led up to an incident, as well as the ripples that result from the incident, come from and move on into infinity, crossing every life, every city, state, country, and ultimately far beyond. An act of charity in a Midwestern American town can be felt as far away as Tokyo. Likewise, an act of terror in Europe can ripple across the Atlantic and find itself sitting in the pews of an old church in the Bronx.

There is absolutely no escaping the law of cause and effect, or the fact that humanity is connected not only through the same Spirit of God, but by a series of events as well. Take a moment to look at your life. Look at your past and plot out exactly how you've come to be in this moment. Look at the lives that have affected yours and vice versa, and how those lives affect other lives, and on and on and on. No, this is not a new concept. There are hundreds, if not thousands, of books that say this. So why am I repeating it? Because I still run into people on a regular basis who just don't get it. Don't get that life is about experiencing the effects of your choices, learning and growing from them, and understanding the beauty of the one law that governs the universe (gods, angels, and human beings alike).

And as I said above, angels don't work within the realm of what makes us happy or sad or comfortable or uncomfortable, or in terms of what we consider good or bad. These are all human constructs in which the angels are not contained. In obeying the law of causality, the angels are motivated by purpose and purpose alone: your purpose. This is not to say they work without compassion or without love. Quite the opposite. It is through compassion for we who desire this human experience, and out of love for us as sisters and brothers in spirit, that the angels operate the way they do.

Let's examine this concept through a story that you are most likely familiar with. Let us look at Judas Iscariot. This man is probably one of the most hated in human history. A historical icon of evil and greed, Judas will forever be known as the disciple who betrayed Jesus Christ with a kiss, thus beginning the Messiah's long, arduous journey to his crucifixion. Let's look at that a moment.

The very cornerstone of Christianity is the crucifixion of Christ. Without the crucifixion, also known as the Perfect Sacrifice, there is no atonement for sins; there is no sacrifice good enough to pay for the transgressions of humankind. In short, if it weren't for Judas who betrayed Christ, would Jesus have gone down in history simply as a Jewish mystic who claimed he was the son of God only to be silenced by old age and death? Can one dare entertain a world without Christ? Without the crucifixion? Without Christianity? (Or Judaism? or Buddhism? or Earth-based beliefs?)

Though Christians are quick to revere the death of Christ (and I say death because without death there is no resurrection), the role that Judas played is often overlooked, if not misconstrued altogether. In one breath, Judas is the betrayer; in another breath, Christ's death heals our sins. Judas is evil; Christ is good. What sane person would argue about this?

Well, I've always questioned my sanity, so let me take a stab at it. Based on the information provided to me by the angels, we all write our life's scripts before we enter the human realm. That being the case, could we not conjecture that somewhere in Heaven, during the great gathering of angels where Christ announced he was incarnating as man, that Christ already wrote the crucifixion into his script? If so, then who would take the fall? Judas stepped up to volunteer and so became defamed as one of the cruelest and most misguided souls known to history.

I have often heard Christian leaders denounce Judas, casting the man to the depths of Hell every Easter Sunday for betraying Christ. At the risk of compromising my credibility, I have to chuckle a bit. Judas in Hell? Hardly. This is not to say he did not experience a personal hell when he returned home to the realm of Spirit. The angels channeled visions to me of Judas wrought with grief and regret—even as he walked among them, even as he walked by Christ's side. And as Judas languished in the memories of what happened to Christ because of his betrayal, his spiritual family endured his gloom. The angels walked with him, consoling him and constantly reminding him of what his spiritual identity was: not a betrayer of Light, but a brother and a heavenly volunteer whom God trusted was strong enough to carry out the plan set forth for Christ—a plan that not even the angels were willing to volunteer for.

There was a purpose to be served. Judas offered himself up to help fulfill that purpose for the birth and glory of a new religion called Christianity. His purpose was not to be evil or loathsome, but to act as a catalyst, a cause to bring about a desired effect—the crucifixion of Jesus of Nazareth.

So am I saying that we should have sympathy for the Devil? No. Firstly, Judas is no devil. Secondly, he doesn't need our sympathy. Like everyone else in the world who has been deemed malevolent—Hitler, Saddam Hussein, Manson, Dahmer, etc.—Judas served a purpose. We all have a purpose to fulfill, but some of us are willing to wear masks of wickedness in order to act as mirrors of our world's social ills, our short-falls, our inability to take responsibility for our own actions. Souls of this ilk descend upon us, create causes, and return home to spirit. Some return unscathed, understanding the purpose they served. Others, like Judas, carry back with them immeasurable burdens of guilt and shame that will not allow them peace in the realm of spirit. Such souls are then redirected, to a realm where the angels work closely with them to help them heal. One might consider this realm a type of Hell or Purgatory, but it is not an eternal place of torment administered by demons and devils. The torment comes from within the soul itself. When the soul is able to let go of the guilt or anger or malice or any other human emotion that weighs a spirit down, then it is free to return home to where all souls go, to the bosom of God, to the Source of All That Is.

When burdened souls like this walk among us, when the world faces an evil, change is brought about: nations unify, governments take action, economies are affected, people are affected—cause and effect. Some may argue that such changes can be for the better or worse, but as I tell my clients, this again takes us back to the rudimentary constructs that hinder our progress as spiritual beings: good versus bad.

So why do we cling to such notions as good and bad? Initially, it is a way to protect our boundaries, a way to separate "us" from "them." But most importantly, it is a way to gain or maintain power. Humans have always feared the unknown. We fear what we do not understand—hence the fear of God, war, terrorism, the enemy. Where there is ignorance, there is fear. Where there is the illusion that "there is not enough," there is fear and greed. Where there is no understanding that every human being is connected to each other through the Source of Creation, there is no respect for the lives of "them" in comparison to our own lives. The mentality of "my god is bigger than your god" is born, creating a breeding ground for dissension and hate.

If we instead take responsibility for our lives, as the creators or authors of our circumstances, and accept with impartiality that everything "just is," then the notions of good and evil fall to the wayside. Anger and hate are diffused, and all that is left are the lessons we all were put here to learn. The ex-spouse whose face you plastered on the family dartboard made an agreement with you to play the villain when you authored your life, to teach you through experience how to deal with issues such as codependence, self-esteem, or anger. The boss who seems to have made it his business to make your life a living hell agreed with you before you were born to teach you lessons in self-worth, assertiveness, and setting boundaries. The rowdy roommate who unscrupulously kicked you out of an apartment lease renewal did exactly what she was supposed to do, forcing you to find other living arrangements so that you could learn the importance of quietude and meditation during your spiritual growth.

When we all engage the idea that we are ultimately responsible for our lives—responsible for every experience we have—there can be no anger or hate... because there is no *good* or *evil* or *me* or *them*. There is only your purpose. This is where our connections to our angels, spirit guides, and ascended masters come in. They can help us process these experiences and learn our spiritual lessons, so we are not blindly caught up in our egos, our pride, or our illusions of what "should be."

When we seek these connections with the angels, we are seeking understanding and freedom from our illusions of comfort. As long as life is "good," we are complacent and inert, hopelessly dependent on a false sense of security and peace. When life becomes turbulent, we are kinetic forces desperately trying to bring order to our lives—and to ultimately create another illusion of comfort. But after so many bouts with disillusion, we will finally get to a place where we no longer

seek more illusions to appease, but rather cling to the truth of "what will be, will be."

When we begin to view life through this truth, then we can see life as neither good nor bad, but as a spiritual lesson in (insert your lesson of choice here). Life becomes a series of experiences from which we can gain great knowledge of our most inner workings as human beings. To tap into that knowledge is to connect with all living things. To connect with all living things is to connect to our angels, ambassadors of God who is the Source of all Creation. To connect to the Source of all Creation is to know the Source of all Creation. And finally, to know the Source of all Creation is to know your Self, your highest Self unbound and unlimited, free of pride, ego, and illusions. To know your Self is to be fully awake and aware of all things as they exist within you, through you, and all around you.

But before we launch into a wild romp through the angelic realms, I want you to understand up front that even though working with your angels will lead to some of the most awe-inspiring experiences ever, you have to do your part, too. What is your part? Acceptance. We're so willing to accept angels as our spiritual handymen who come to fix the broken doors and windows of our lives, but when they point out that the broken window isn't causing the draft—it's the fact that you're missing an entire side of your house (and here's the estimate)—then we buckle and retreat, cheating ourselves out of valuable lessons, the necessary repairs that will give us the rock solid foundation upon which to build our spiritual lives.

I always tell clients that spiritual growth is like resistance training. This is the type of training where you work against the forces of gravity to build up muscles in your body. The greater the resistance, and the harder your body has to work, the stronger your body becomes over time. To live a life without resistance—or adversity—would be like lifting a single feather in an effort to build your biceps. What could you possibly hope to achieve? And so it is with spirituality. If you are going to work with your angels, you must shift how you view your life. Yes, the concept that life operates solely in terms of learning lessons is a hard concept swallow. But I'm not telling you to simply throw caution to the wind because you have no control over events. And I'm certainly not telling you to go about life all willy-nilly because of the notion that *no matter what I do, it won't change my fate anyhow*. God may be in control of our circumstances, our environment, and our fate, but we still have control over how we react to them and how we learn from them. So when adversity comes your way and you've spent two or three nights crying *why me?*, buckle down and put on what I call "angel visors." That is to say, shift how you view life by asking yourself, *how would Michael view this?* Or better yet, *what is Michael up to?* Nothing happens to you by accident. Your angels

know well in advance what's coming your way, and are the conductors during your life challenge.

Ask yourself what lesson can be learned during your moment of crisis. Mind you, the lesson may not reveal itself immediately. It could take days, months, or even years before you understand why your house was the only one on the block leveled by the storm. Just, whatever you do, do not be quick to cry out, "God, why are you punishing me!"

Now, I'll be honest. When tragedy hits, I've been very guilty of making that my first prayer. And then my angel-on-call will whisper, "It's not a punishment. You're all right. Work with what you have and all will be revealed soon enough." Every time, the purpose of a tragedy is revealed, and through that revelation I've grown stronger and wiser. Moreover, I become grateful. That's right, I said *grateful*, for the upset, because every challenge in your life will always bring a gift of significant proportions. This is where the majority of us get lost. We get so wrapped up in our own dramas that we fail to see how God is truly working in our lives. We fail to see the gifts that come attached to our trials.

The saying "When God closes a door, he opens a window" is not just a pretty phrase we use to help keep our spirits up during hard times. It's the truth, through and through! It's just that we're so devastated that the door is closed that we sit and stare at it forever, hoping it will reopen; and all the while, we're completely oblivious to the open window behind us. And we don't even have to shimmy down the drainpipe! We're on the ground floor, but our natural resistance against the unknown—against change—makes us think we're a hundred stories up. We'd rather waste time thinking about "what could have been" than seize the opportunities offered by "what is."

Humans are creatures of survival, and we are also creatures of comfort. We are quick to run from what we perceive as danger, and just as quick to run from what we perceive as an inconvenience. While our angels flank us on all sides twenty-four hours a day, they are not necessarily here to protect us from "bad" things; they are here simply help us face our spiritual trials.

While getting to know your angels, understand that you will continue to face many life challenges. The key to working with them effectively is to ask them, "What is the purpose of all of this? Why would I choose such experiences this lifetime?" Just being mindful that everything that happens is without accident, and with purpose, will help you be more receptive to your angels' guidance—and will make your relationship with them one of encouragement and inspiration.

My hope for all my readers is that you are able to enjoy the company of angels to create a life of awe and wonder. In this world and at this time, humanity needs all the love and understanding it can get. Yes, current events may get you down, but connecting with your angels will lift you up, reminding you that miracles still happen. Angels are written into our life scripts to encourage us and propel us along our life paths. Need proof of a miracle? Look in the mirror.

You are a miracle in progress, my friend.

> *Science of Mind teaches that there is a favorable physical*
> *reaction, an effect, which follows a pattern of thought*
> *incorporating ideas of health, for the law of cause*
> *and effect governs everything.*
> —Ernest Holmes

MY INTERVIEWS
WITH THE ANGELS

O ne afternoon while sitting at my computer, I found an email innocently waiting in my mailbox. It was a forwarded message, a dreaded chain letter with about four FWDs preceding the subject header. I hate chain letters, but I decided to open this one, and after scrolling through about a hundred email addresses of those too lazy to copy and paste the letter into a blank email, I came across one of those surveys. You know the type—the "get to know your friend better" chain letter with a dozen or so questions about your likes and dislikes.

My first thought was to just delete the email and reply to my friend, "We've known each other for ten years! If you don't know the answers to these questions by now, God help us both. Lovingly, Chantel."

But instead, I looked across the table at Michael, who was kicking back and enjoying the summer sun coming in through the window of my consultation room. An impish grin crossed my lips and the conversation went a bit like this:

"Hey, Mike?"

"Yeap?"

"What's your favorite color?"

"My hair, why?"

"Oh, just wondered." I chuckled, and then proceeded to ask him the rest of the questions in the survey. In hindsight, I realize that his asking me "why?" was simply for appearances. He could have just answered and been done with it, especially since (through his angelic knowledge) he knew that the email had landed in my mailbox and would provoke such a response from me. But this illustrates just how eager the angels are to engage with us directly, to fully be a part of this life's experience. His very presence in the room helped, too. If we hadn't been talking only minutes prior, I would have disregarded my friend's email and thought nothing more of it. But out of curiosity, and perhaps even a bit of boredom, I decided to have a little fun that afternoon with a charming, fun-loving jokester of an angel and see how he would respond to the questionnaire.

Still, the afternoon was just that—a brief moment in my existence that I thought nothing much about once it was over. I saved my interview with Michael among my countless computer files, and it vanished from my memory. It wasn't until Archangel Raphael came to me about writing a book, a year later, that I thought about the interview with Michael and wondered what could develop from it.

The angel profiles you will read in this book were inspired not only by that wayward email, but by the MySpace phenomenon as well (of which I feel too old to be a part of, for some reason). This social networking website, and others like it, is a voyeur's paradise. It seems that the majority of the MySpace crowd is perfectly fine with sharing information as mundane as a favorite rock band or summer blockbuster film, or as intimate as a favorite type of kiss or secret ticklish spot. While I wasn't inclined to ask Michael whether he preferred boxers or briefs beneath his battle armor, I *was* curious about a few other things. I tried to imagine what his MySpace page would look like . . .

Blaring music, swirling psychedelic colors, and rogue html code aside, the drive behind the angel profiles was my desire to get to know my friends better. In this case, those friends have been and always will be the archangels. When I proposed the idea to them, many were on board immediately, Michael and Gabriel being the first two. Others I had to hunt down: Uriel, Raguel, and Ramiel. And some quietly waited in the rafters, intermittently tossing down a random glimpse into their hearts whenever I was receptive to it.

EXPLANATION OF THE PROFILE FORMAT

If I've said it once, I've said it a thousand times: there is no such thing as coincidence. While the editor was working on the final draft of this book, she asked me why I had chosen the order I had for the list of angels. I'd struggled a bit with this; since all the angels have equal powers, I wanted to avoid listing them by hierarchy (although Michael would have loved it), but if I listed them alphabetically, Azrael—the angel of death—was first on the list. I worried that those of you who have yet to encounter the dark angel and experience his compassionate nature might be a bit rattled to start off with Azrael. So, my list was a bit alphabetical, and a bit content-driven. What's an angel medium to do?

Well, literally days before I got the question, I discovered quite "by accident" a neat little quirk: these twelve archangels (whom I'd initially chosen because I work with them on a regular basis) can be divided into four subgroups: the Nurturers, the Warriors, the Workers, and the Intercessors.

The Nurturers are the angels who come into our lives to help us feel better about ourselves and to motivate us to make beneficial decisions—not only about our spiritual bodies, but about our physical bodies, too. This group includes Chamuel, Iophiel, and Raphael.

The Warriors are those who go to battle for us and offer up words of encouragement to bolster our faith in Heaven—and more importantly, our faith in ourselves. These are the heavenly gladiators who jump into the fray, wielding their swords to defend us and provide a sense of security along our spiritual journey. This group includes Michael, Uriel, and Cassiel.

The Workers don't always interact closely with humanity, preferring instead to act behind the scenes. But they are always happy to help if called upon. They hold great knowledge, and have access to every morsel of information God is willing to share. These angels won't hesitate to appear in your life when it's time for you to get down to business and tend to life issues. This group includes Metatron, Raguel, and Ramiel.

And finally, there are the Intercessors. These angels interact with us more closely than the others. They not only deliver messages to us from Heaven, but also hear our prayers and carry our requests up to the celestial throne. Basically, they're Heaven's telephone company and courier service. The group includes Gabriel, Sandalphon, and Azrael.

Within each angel's profile, I've divided my discussion into three parts: a questionnaire, a description of the angel's "mansion" in the heavenly realms, and an "angel manifest" section that gives a general overview of the angel's purpose and potential role in your life.

The questionnaire, of course, asks the angel some basic questions, like their favorite color or favorite type of music. But I was not only curious about the mundane; I also wanted to know if the angels had any particular views or opinions about the world and its inhabitants. I quickly found out that in addition to having some very strong opinions about humanity as a whole, the angels want to share their opinions and insights, both serious and light-hearted, for the people of the world to ponder. You might find yourself agreeing with a few angels and their perspectives; and you might find yourself disagreeing. The point of this section is not to sway you toward any particular view. In fact, Michael informed me right from the beginning that "people are going to believe what they *need* to believe, regardless of what you, we, and anyone else say."

What Michael means by this is that, because we are all here to fulfill a purpose, we are only going to agree with and accept ideals, paradigms, and concepts that serve as catalysts to get us from one point of our experience to the next. Take my experience with Archangel Chamuel, for example. He is the protector of nature—the trees, the rivers and streams, the mountains and all that's in between. Well, this also includes animals, and while he did not come right out and express his views about people who eat meat, I felt a heavy sense of guilt while interviewing him. Afterwards, I sat at my computer for days, pondering whether to become a vegetarian. And while plenty of my friends and associates would love it if I turned away from turkey tetrazzini to a Gardenburger instead, I just cannot do that at this time. I'm a big gal, born of two proud Southern parents whose philosophy was,

"If we can fry it in Crisco, we can eat it." Old habits die hard, and it's not that I haven't tried being a vegetarian. I have—and with long-term success in the past—but dang it all, sometimes a girl's just gotta have a nice, hulkin' piece of USDA grade A, corn-fed beef—a medium-grilled porterhouse, thank you.

Of course, after Chamuel's interview, I thought twice about poor Betsy the Cow's life on the farm, but cravings for tenderloin medallions with shallots and garlic butter won out. One friend quipped that with every animal I consume, I'm racking up bad karma, and she would probably be happy to know that Chamuel is on her side when it comes to eating animals. Luckily for me, I don't believe in bad karma, but since I was feeling additional guilt from her constant nagging, I had gone to the Archangel with a whiny protest, anyhow.

"You are who you are, Chantel," Chamuel said calmly, sitting in a lotus pose in the middle of one of his many gardens. He has the demeanor of a serene, wise sage, and prefers to sit in meditation whenever we connect.

"Yeah, so I hear. Still, Chamuel, is it wrong or not?"

"Depends on the reality you have chosen for yourself."

"That doesn't answer my question, great kung-fu master," I grumbled back at him.

"To eat meat, or not to eat meat, is not the question. The question is, who are you and what is your purpose?

"What the heck does that have to do with my choosing baby back ribs over a salad?"

"Everything . . . and nothing at all."

I stood with my hands on my hips, weight on one foot, nostrils flared. There Chamuel sat, just as tranquil as the stream flowing quietly by him. I felt like a lion—I wanted to pounce on the angel and beat a straightforward answer out of him.

"I'm okay with it." I nodded briskly. "I'm cool. No problem. No guilt."

"You sure about that?"

"Dang it, Cham! Look, let's just forget we had this conversation."

"What conversation?" He never moved. Even as a breeze enveloped us, his robes and his hair remained still.

I stormed out of the meditation and sat at my computer, tapping my nails in frustration on the keyboard. I look at it like this: I've already made the choice to eat a Quarter Pounder rather than stir-fried tofu, right? I just have to understand what that choice means. Maybe my life script ends at fifty-five instead of eighty-five. With the way I eat, I'm right on schedule.

And so it may be for you—what the angels have to say about humanity, or life in general, may lead you to ponder your own place in this world and what your choices mean. (Or you may simply say, *Chantel's a nutcase. What angel would say that?* And that's perfectly fine, too. I've been called worse.)

Also, there are two items in each questionnaire that I want to clarify before we moved ahead: *Ascended Masters and Benevolent Spirit Teachers with similar energy signatures,* and *Notable people with similar vibration*.

The first item contains the names of ascended masters, as well as deities from religions around the world. As I mentioned in the Frequently Asked Questions about Angels chapter, the angels are not bound by religion or beliefs, only by purpose (God's direction). They have taken on many forms throughout history and continue to do so in the modern age, but the fact that a deity, ascended master, or the muse behind a myth is listed in an angel's questionnaire does not necessarily mean that it is an incarnation of that particular angel. It simply means that the energies are similar in nature. It is also not meant to debase a master, deity, or religion; it is simply a way of illustrating how vast, creative, and all-encompassing the Spirit realm is.

Keep in mind that while you may talk philosophy with Gabriel, or ask Michael for strength, what you are connecting with is the Source of those angels—a Source that is spread out across the infinite universe and has innumerable names. You can liken this phenomenon to a network where you have to log in to a server; the angel's Source is like the server, and the actual angel (ascended master, etc.) is similar to your computer. Your computer's name may be "Gabriel." Someone in the Middle East

may use the name "Djibril" for their computer. Someone in the Far East may use "Buddha." My personal favorite is "Jesus."

In the second item, *Notable people with similar vibration*, you will find a handful of public figures whose life force matches the angel's vibration. This in no way infers that the people on the list are angels themselves or even that their lives were filled with angelic deeds (though there's a few I'd like to think might have a shot at sainthood one day). The point of this section is to illustrate the many faces of the angels, and henceforth of the Creator itself. Some of these people you may like, others you may not, but that's irrelevant, really. The point is to understand that we are all embodiments of the Spirit, and whether we like the vessels in which the Spirit comes or not, we must acknowledge that there is a higher purpose for its existence and strive to understand that purpose.

You may even look at a list and say, "Wow, what about what's-his-name? How come he isn't on here?" It's not that I've intentionally left anyone out. The lists could go on forever. But for the sake of my sanity, I could name only so many people. Feel free to send me suggestions concerning any I've missed!

The next section of each profile looks at the angel's mansion. These offer a peek into the place where each angel hangs out when things are a bit slow (oh, like that ever happens). There is a colossal, city-like structure that I got the privilege of touring on a few occasions, thanks to Gabriel; within this structure, there is a mansion (for lack of a better word) assigned to each archangel. "Breathtaking" is a gross understatement when describing the magnitude and beauty of each residence. I doubt I will ever find words adequate to describe the houses of the angels, but hopefully this section will give you another perspective into their unique personalities.

Let me give you a quick back story as to how I discovered the angelic mansions.

A few years ago, my life was becoming turbulent (that's putting it lightly). I'd left my job of seven years based on the advice of a spirit guide (who was later backed up by Archangel Gabriel and a handful of "coincidences"). I had left the job in June—but instead of enjoying the summer as Gabriel, with his sparkly blue eyes, encouraged me to do, I shifted into a mode of complete panic. I had enough money saved up to live on until the following spring, as long as nothing catastrophic happened. But my $500 COBRA payments, my $300 car note, and my $900 house note were ever-present. I began to worry, for I realized I hadn't quite planned out this leap of faith as well as I thought I had. In a nutshell, I was skydiving without a parachute.

Day and night, I was busy hunting for a new job, writing and rewriting résumés to fit whatever position I was applying for. I mailed out dozens of résumés only to be met with silence. My phone never rang, and bills continued to eat away at my savings.

"Chantel, the job you receive does not require a résumé," Gabriel quietly whispered as I sat at my altar and prayed fervently for new employment. I didn't listen to him, instead stepped up my résumé production line, seeking any and all available employment.

I found myself yelling at my angelic guide for dragging me into this new hell. I say "new" because my former job was a hell unto itself—but at least I could count on a paycheck every Friday. And this was my thinking as I spouted off curses and screamed to God, "Why do you hate me so much? I do what you ask and strife is what I get?" I had spent many a sleepless night thinking about how all that I had found peace and security in was quickly slipping through my fingers: my home, my car, my health insurance, my internet service provider.

Finally one day, while sitting in a local park, I made a determination to pick yet another bone with God. It wouldn't be the first time I'd lodged a formal and most irate complaint with Him. I had even told Gabriel about my intention to do this. The golden-haired angel smirked and said, "Go right ahead."

I must admit I wasn't expecting such a casual response from Gabriel, who is usually quite formal, if not solemn. If anything, I was expecting to get struck by lightning right there in the sunshine by the park fountain. (I was silently hoping, anyway. It'd be hard for my car's financing company to find my new address on Other Side Avenue.) But he'd given me the go-ahead to complain, so I let loose.

I got home that evening and sat in my family room. The neighborhood was blissfully quiet. I contemplated my harsh words earlier and felt myself shrinking sheepishly with each passing minute. *I just challenged God. Oh, crap.* I hadn't quite finished the thought before Gabriel appeared beside me with a grin.

"You ready?" he asked. "Wouldn't want you to be late for your appointment."

"No, I'm not ready."

"Well, you're the one who initiated this. Who said God doesn't fill requests?"

"Shut up."

"Move it, Chantel. Let's go."

"I'm hungry. I need to eat something so my stomach doesn't growl while I'm busy complaining."

"Fine, eat and let's go."

I stalled for as long as I could, like a child nibbling at dinner to avoid bath time and bedtime for as long as possible. And Gabriel, like the mother he can often be, nudged me and said, "You've had enough. Get going."

Grudgingly, I sat in the living room in my mother's favorite high-back chair, did my breathing exercises, and then slipped (albeit hesitantly) into meditation. My steps inward were part of a customized method, a basic chakra walk-through I'd developed while learning Reiki. It was there that I met up with Gabriel again, who then guided me into a room so white and so bright that I could not discern the walls from the floor.

"I can't go back?" I stood before him.

"They're waiting for you." Suddenly, a door appeared beside the angel and I approached it with trepidation.

"They? I'm gonna die, aren't I?"

"Chantel, stop it. Do not be afraid. I am right beside you," Gabriel whispered, and right before my eyes he transformed to a white mist, leaving only a pair of shiny onyx eyes for me to focus on. I yelped in shock and clutched my chest in fear.

"Gabe?"

"Chantel, it's all right."

I wanted to cry; I had that feeling you get right before stepping onto a heart-stopping, anti-gravity, oh-my-god-I'm-gonna-die roller coaster. There was enough adrenaline flowing through me to resurrect King Tut.

"I changed my mind. I wanna go back," I whined as I peered into the darkness beyond the door.

Gabriel gave me the heave-ho.

"Hello?" I called out, hearing my own voice reply in a light echo. I spun around a few times, finding myself in a room as dark as the white room had been bright. Fear began to fill me and I began to regret that I had opened my big mouth earlier at the park.

Though it seemed like forever, it really was only a few seconds before something broke the veil of darkness. No, it wasn't an old bearded man on a throne, or a young bearded man on a cross, or a golden-skinned man sitting on a lotus flower. Instead, a group of twelve bodies of light suddenly came into view—as if they had been there the whole time. Their bodies were formless, and pulsed and hummed. Radiating a warm glow of gold and white, they looked like strange jellyfish—beautiful wisps of tendrils left trails of gold particles with each graceful move.

"I do not understand what it is you want from me." My voice was meek. I wanted to bow my head simply out of propriety, but the vision before me was so breathtaking, there was no way I could avert my eyes.

"It is not about what we want, but what *you* want, Chantel." The twelve lights spoke in one resounding voice and seemed to be more in my head than around me. And then, as if by instinct, I found myself speaking to them telepathically. As I did so, Gabriel's human form appeared, gestured for my attention, and then pointed back at me. I looked down at myself to see that my body now had transformed into that same ethereal, golden glow. The exchange between us all now was fantastical, but I wanted to be afraid. I felt that I should be, at the very least, fearful that I was dreaming all of this and that this was all an elaborate play upon my imagination. Yet I couldn't feel fear. It was as if I had forgotten what fear felt like, altogether. I could not feel doubt, either.

"What *I* want?" I echoed the lights. "I did not ask for this. I just want happiness. I need a job right now. I'm so worried about my finances." Yes, that was how shallow I used to be. Here I was experiencing what few humans ever experience and all I could worry about was my cable-television payments.

"But you did ask for this. Remember, Chantel. Remember why you are here. Remember your purpose."

"Purpose? What purpose? Wait, this makes no sense. I'm nobody! Why are you making me go through this?"

"We are not. We explained to you the consequences of choosing this path. Now you must follow it to the end."

Vexed and flustered, I looked at Gabriel's luminous form. He must have sensed my distress and moved closer to me. "I will do whatever it is I am put here to do, but I seek your guidance. I feel so lost," I moaned.

"You were not nor have you ever been lost. You have simply forgotten who you are." With that, the lights faded. I wanted to chase after them, but I felt mentally exhausted by the whole thing. And I hadn't even gotten a chance to speak my mind, really.

"Want to go on a tour?" Gabriel's warmth enveloped me.

"Where are we?" I looked around the darkness. Gabriel ascended toward the spot where the twelve lights had hovered.

"Come on," he whispered to my mind, and I effortlessly followed him, hoping that if I remembered how to fly, I could remember why I was living the life I had chosen.

The darkness around us soon gave way to bright, sunlit skies. I followed Gabriel's form to a glistening metropolis made of silver, gold, and crystal. I could not see the ground, and the city seemed to hover in the sky with its tall skyscrapers and nestled buildings. If anything, it looked fantastically high-tech.

And then I saw them, the city's inhabitants: thousands, perhaps tens of thousands, of luminous beings. These bodies of light shone brightly as they swirled about each other like a bloom of jellyfish in a dazzling blue sea. As Gabriel and I hovered for a moment, I noticed a thin strand of electrical current that connected each body of light to the others like a golden umbilical cord. It was only when I looked at Gabriel again that I noticed that we, too, were connected.

I felt him smile at me, and he descended toward the city. I followed him. We were suddenly in the flow of things, moving about with the other luminous bodies, moving in and out of buildings, communicating, feeling, hearing everything. I could hear thousands of voices all at once, and instinctively knew that I could choose to listen to them all, or to just one, or to none at all.

I was completely engaged in the moment, trying to view and then file everything in my mind for playback at some point. Then, at Gabriel's urging, we ascended once again—but not before I saw something truly magnificent happen. I witnessed two bodies of light moving toward each other. They seemed to regard each other a moment, and then merged into one body.

Instinctively, I opened my connection through the umbilical cord for a second to feel what those two souls felt, and was overwhelmed by what I knew was love. But as I watched the single body of light move into the distance, I realized it was so much more than that. It was a complete merging of souls, something far more intense than what humans could achieve or even possibly fathom. I lingered there a moment, until I could see the merged soul no more and Gabriel tugged on me to follow him once again.

We entered a great corridor with heavier traffic and then veered off into another corridor where the walls were lined with what looked like old-fashioned post office boxes. The walls towered up into infinity, it seemed.

"What is this?"

"What does it look like?" Gabriel led the way as we wove between countless other souls.

"A post office." I chuckled and hovered closer to the wall. The boxes had a script on them that I couldn't read at first, but suddenly it faded into long strands of numbers. "Hey, do I have a box here?"

"Where do you think I'm taking you?" Gabriel grumbled back at me.

"Hey, don't get snippy. I'm human. I forgot this was here."

After a short trek, he led me to a box. There was no need for a key. I simply opened it and started sifting through ... junk.

Drawings, scrolls of parchment. It looked like a junk drawer from the kitchen. Major disappointment. I was hoping to find a check from Ed McMahon, but no such luck.

I'm not sure how long I stayed there, sifting through a box that seemingly had no end to it, but when I looked up, Gabriel was nowhere to be found. My first emotion was concern, but it quickly gave way to curiosity. I looked around a moment and figured that if Gabriel wanted to find me, he could. With that, I went exploring.

I soon found myself traveling in areas with much less traffic and just moseyed along, taking in the sights. For some reason, however, I was compelled to keep going upward, and when I did I quickly became a child in a toy store without parental supervision. I encountered a massive structure of gold, limestone, and crystal. It looked like the Roman Colosseum, but it was intact and immaculate and soared so high into the sky that I had to strain to see the gold dome at the top. This megalith was hundreds of times bigger than any modern sports stadium, and had more levels than I could count. At first, I expected to find human souls dwelling in it, but as I ventured freely in and out of the open suites (two on each level), I quickly came to the realization that these lavish abodes belonged to the archangels. They are the angelic mansions.

Even the enormity of the building hadn't prepared me for what I found inside. The suites aren't just fancy living quarters;

they're entire worlds unto themselves, worlds created and governed by the angels, worlds that welcome visiting souls. (Well, some suites are more welcoming that others, as you'll find out later.) For comparison, think of Disney's World Showcase at Epcot. But rather than man-made pavilions representing different countries and cultures, which together span a few acres of land, each angelic mansion is its own separate reality—a mini universe that not only displays each angel's personal tastes, but also illustrates the immeasurable scope of their creative power.

Now, while many of you may think that this was all just a fanciful play of the imagination, let me say that initially I thought the same thing. When Gabriel found me and led me homeward, I asked him to validate the meditation.

"Help me with my past-due car note, and I'll buy that this actually happened today."

"Give it time," he responded simply. "Until then, I must ask you to do me one big favor."

Gabriel was asking me for a favor? Now I knew I was dreaming! But I answered, "For you, Gabe, anything!"

"Good." He took me by the shoulders. "I need you to get out of my way."

"Get out of your way? You can walk through walls and you want me to get out of your way? You got it." I chuckled dryly.

"I'm serious, Chantel. I need to work here and I need you to not do anything."

"Oh, you mean stop posting resumes and doing that job search thing? I'll tell you what, Gabe, if you get my car note paid, I'll believe this happened *and* I'll stop looking for a job."

With a grumble, Gabriel's eyes narrowed to thin slits and he walked away, leading me out of the meditation.

When I opened my eyes in my living room, I became dizzy. The room spun. I tried to stand up, but it felt as if I had just gotten out of the swimming pool and was feeling the pull of Earth's gravity again. Within minutes I was sick to my stomach, and I spent the evening trying to fight off the nausea. I stayed in the chair for another two hours.

The sun was setting, bathing the living room in a deep, amber glow. I didn't understand what had just happened. For all I knew, the whole meditation was just been one heck of a daydream. But the physical effects were anything but figments of an overactive imagination. I felt as if I were underwater—everything looked different. The same, but different. I was exceedingly aware of everything around me. Hours later, the shock of gravity and my keener awareness evolved into a deep depression, and I retreated up to my bedroom.

I had seen it—the Source of All That Is. I had touched it, connected with it. My thoughts seemed to be stuck on *repeat*. I felt that I didn't deserve the experience, that there were so many others in the world far more deserving than I. Still, I was grateful for it, even if it was just a dream and although it only raised more questions than answers. And naturally, I still had my doubts. Would the angel keep his end of the deal and prove to me that it wasn't just a fanciful play of sleep, imagination, and a heavy meal?

Twenty-four hours later, an unexpected email appeared in my mailbox. It was from PayPal, notifying me of a money transfer. Not just any money transfer, but one to the tune of $3500. Attached was a note from a friend in London: *Chantel, I know you recently quit your job and I know it may seem a bit harrowing to take this leap of faith, so I hope this gift helps quell some of your doubts. I believe in you even if you don't yet believe in yourself.*

Coincidence, maybe?

The last section in each angel profile describes how the angels manifest in our lives—how they manifested to me, and how and when they might manifest to you. I hope this section helps bring everything you've read together, and encourages you to watch for that angel in your life.

You are now cordially invited to take a peek into the lives and personalities of each of the archangels. This project has really helped me get to know the angels and their lovable personalities better. With all my heart and soul, I hope that the following pages will inspire you to connect with your angels, so that your spirit might be uplifted and encouraged. The angels are waiting! Don't be shy—jump right in and discover for yourself just how wondrous and witty they can be.

ARCHANGEL
CHAMUEL

A NURTURER

The breath of Chamuel is peace.
The breath of Chamuel is balance.

—Archangel Sandalphon

———+———

Meaning of name: He who sees [seeks] God.

Trivia: Also known as *Camael*, Chamuel has been associated with the god of war in Druid mythology and also is said to be the angel in the Garden of Gethsemane.

Message to the contemporary world: To make peace with yourself is to make peace with the world.

Patron angel (traditionally) of: Warriors, hunters and gatherers, farmers, protectors and preservationists of Nature.

Patron angel (currently) of: Horticulturists, hunters (non-recreational), outdoor survivalists, physical fitness trainers, forest rangers, gardeners, farmers, chefs and cooks, naturalists, environmentalists, philanthropists, emergency aid workers.

Ruler of: Thursday (Jupiter); co-rules with Ramiel.

HEAVENLY ASSIGNMENT: Oversees the balance and order of nature. Chamuel is also instrumental in helping humankind understand its connection with the planet Earth.

DEMEANOR WHEN ON THE JOB: Mild mannered.

DEMEANOR WHEN AT PLAY: Chamuel is a meditative angel, and prefers to dwell in the many forests on our planet. Though highly focused, he never hesitates to offer a smile of approval to those who respect nature and themselves.

HUMAN ACCOMPLISHMENTS MOST PROUD OF: Earth Day, if only humans paid more attention to it.

BACK IN THE DAY, HE LIKED: A person's childlike wonder when they realize just how important all creatures are in the natural order of life.

TODAY, HE ENJOYS: The same.

PET PEEVE: Hunting for trophies.

HOPE FOR THE WORLD (SERIOUS): For it to understand that the phrase "all life is precious" doesn't just apply to humans and their pets.

HOPE FOR THE WORLD (WHIMSICAL): "Humans always have separated themselves from the animal kingdom on the basis that humans use tools. Well, now that this division has crumbled in light of recent discoveries, what will humans think of next to vainly keep themselves at the top of the food chain? To help you all, let me clarify that the argument against animals having no souls or having the inability to recognize God is a step in the wrong direction."

IF HE HAD AN ASTROLOGICAL SIGN, IT WOULD BE: Capricorn.

ELEMENTS: Earth, trees, mountains, foliage.

GEMSTONES WITH SIMILAR VIBRATION: Agate, amber, crystal quartz, peridot.

FAVORITE SEASON(S): All seasons.

ANIMAL TOTEM(S): All animals.

WING COLOR: Brown, the wings of an eagle.

FAVORITE ATTIRE: Usually wears a cloak of dark brown or hunter green. May take on the form of the "Green Man," a Buddhist monk, a shaman, a Native American warrior, or an Aborigine elder.

FAVORITE COLOR(S): Earth tones.

FAVORITE FOOD(S): The autumn harvest.

FAVORITE MUSIC: Thunderstorms, tribal drums.

IDEAL DATE: Yoga by a bubbling brook, followed by fruits, nuts, and cheeses for lunch.

ASCENDED MASTERS AND BENEVOLENT SPIRIT TEACHERS WITH SIMILAR ENERGY SIGNATURES: Abundantia, Aine, Artemis, Butterfly Maiden, Diana, Gaia, Green Man, Kokopelli, Pan, St. Francis, Taras (Green and White), Vila.

NOTABLE PEOPLE WITH SIMILAR VIBRATION: Ansel Adams, Bono, Chief Sitting Bull (Tatanka Iyotaka), Luisa Diogo, Jane Goodall, Julia Butterfly Hill, Steve "Crocodile Hunter" Irwin, Amelia Kinkade, Jet Li, Pocahontas.

FAVORITE CONTEMPORARY FICTIONAL CHARACTERS: Rubeus Hagrid, Treebeard.

USUALLY ARRIVES IN YOUR LIFE: When you are facing challenges in staying true to yourself and your cause.

CHAMUEL'S MANSION

Chamuel's world is nature, and his mansion sits within the granddaddy of all Zen gardens.

As I walked in peaceful meditation through Chamuel's mansion, I was soothed by the sound of bubbling brooks and the beauty of meticulously manicured trees and flowerbeds against a breathtaking backdrop of snow-capped mountains. It was a haven of tranquility.

Inside Chamuel's humble abode, with its wide open spaces and minimalist décor, the air was sweet and brisk. I could easily see that the angel spent little time indoors, preferring instead to commune with the teeming life outdoors, in the sunshine. As I stood at the door of the dojo, looking out over the gardens, I spotted several deer leaping playfully about in the distance. Just as I was about to follow them, I was stopped by a little gray hare who hopped into my path and demanded petting. Well, who can resist furry baby bunnies? For the rest of the meditation, I bunny-sat, taking in the serenity I had always felt in the presence of Archangel Chamuel.

It wasn't until the meditation was over that I realized I hadn't explored the grounds as much as I would have liked. But I'm sure that was Chamuel's intention, given that his nature is stillness. I have no doubt that he was teaching me to enter his mansion and simply take pleasure in being there—in the experience itself. I've realized that I don't always have to visit the angels' homes with a specific mission, or even a deadline. The mansions (especially Chamuel's) are a refuge—places that are always open to all who want to breathe in the archangels' presence and feel their strength, power, and love in full force.

It was through stillness that I actually came upon many an interesting discovery about Chamuel's mansion. You never know what treasures of nature you might find in his gardens, but one thing is certain: you will find a sense of peace, come to understand the grandness and beauty of God's Creation, and witness firsthand the brilliance behind the delicate balance between natural forces.

CHAMUEL MANIFEST

Whenever Chamuel shows up in the foreground of a consultation, I know instantly what type of client I'm dealing with. He or she is socially and environmentally conscious, and an activist if only by way of email petitions and armchair politics. Chamuel encourages us to stay true to ourselves and our cause when it is for the inherent good of all. He teaches us that our environment is a reflection of our lives; if we are unhappy with the environment in which we live, we must first change ourselves and our thinking before we try to change others. But even while doing that, should an epiphany come your way, it is not always a license to stand on a soapbox and preach action and move the masses.

Instead, we must follow the example of the very thing Chamuel watches over: nature. Very few things in nature change overnight. To be effective and long-lasting, change must be a gradual process. When change is sharp and forced, you can expect to be met with serious opposition and dissent, whether from your local community when implementing a new ordinance or from your own body when implementing a crash diet.

Chamuel teaches us that patience is a crucial element when seeking change within ourselves and our lives. Again, nature serves as an example. Seeds do not bear fruit within twenty-four hours. They can't even bear fruit within a week, or a month! This is God's way of showing us how to be effective facilitators of change—plant the seed, nurture it and the soil around it. Be diligent and steadfast and allow the seed to do what it is supposed to do in its own good time.

Because we live our lives by the nanosecond, it's difficult for us to allow for gradual change. *We need to take action and, damn it, we need to take it now!* But that's not how the universe works. Even things that seemingly happen overnight took time to germinate. If you're wandering about in your garden and see that a whole new patch of chives has sprouted, the seeds didn't just land there a few days ago. Chances are the wind carried those seeds to the other end of your yard a year ago and they had time to settle in, germinate, take root, and grow.

So, let nature be your teacher when it comes to implementing or even dealing with change. Chamuel is a kind, mild-mannered teacher who comes into our lives when we are seeking to better ourselves—not for vanity's sake, but just because we should be better, period. By bettering ourselves, we set an example for others, facilitating change in our environment. This is a process that requires patience and wisdom, as well as the understanding that we cannot control everything—especially the outcome of our campaign. We do what we can and hope for the best. Does an oak tree begrudge a squirrel for eating acorns? Of course not. The oak tree understands that some of those acorns will take root and turn into great oaks themselves. The father tree isn't worried about the nuts that got away. And you shouldn't be, either.

Change your world by changing yourself first. Ask Chamuel to bring to light those methods that will be most effective for making the changes. Because his presence is so subtle, communicating with Chamuel may require you to engage in quiet meditation or prayer before you receive any noticeable guidance. Find a quiet spot in your garden or a park and allow yourself to commune with nature. Let yourself get lost in the beauty of the trees, the flowers, and the birds. Chamuel's energies flow through all things natural, and it is to those things you should go to truly experience and understand this angel's magnificence.

> *Both the grand and the intimate aspects of nature*
> *can be revealed in the expressive photograph.*
> *Both can stir enduring affirmations and discoveries,*
> *and can surely help the spectator in his search*
> *for identification with the vast world of natural beauty*
> *and the wonder surrounding him.*
>
> —ANSEL ADAMS

ARCHANGEL
RAPHAEL

A NURTURER

Raphael is the best doctor I know.
And he never stepped foot in a medical school.

—Archangel Michael

———+———

Meaning of name: God heals.

Trivia: According to the *Book of Tobit*, Raphael taught Tobias, son of Tobit, how to make medicine from parts of a large fish Tobias caught from a stream. One of the cures was restoring Tobit's sight.

Message to the contemporary world: Heal thyself.

Patron angel (traditionally) of: Astronomers, doctors, healers, nurses, travelers.

Patron angel (currently) of: The above, plus herbalists, intuitives (clairaudients, clairsentients, clairvoyants, claircognants, medical intuitives), light workers (reiki, acupuncture, yoga instructors, massage, kinesiology, chiropractics, etc.), therapists (all types), shamans & medicine women.

Ruler of: Wednesday (Mercury); co-rules with Raguel.

HEAVENLY ASSIGNMENT: To teach and bestow the gifts of healing, intuition, and wisdom.

DEMEANOR WHEN ON THE JOB: Quiet and insightful.

DEMEANOR WHEN AT PLAY: Warm and friendly. A gentle giant.

HUMAN ACCOMPLISHMENTS MOST PROUD OF: Natural medicine.

BACK IN THE DAY, HE LIKED: Innocence.

TODAY, HE ENJOYS: The same. Innocence is the rarest of all gems today.

PET PEEVE: The belief that technological advancement somehow equals social advancement. "They're not even close. In fact, the spiritual evolution of the human race is in retrograde at the moment and has been for centuries. Forward motion will resume in the first half of the twenty-first century."

HOPE FOR THE WORLD (SERIOUS): For it to acknowledge that God's Spirit flows through animals and nature as well as through humans.

HOPE FOR THE WORLD (WHIMSICAL): For it to believe in fairies, unicorns, and other such creatures. As with angels, just because you can't see them doesn't mean they don't exist.

IF HE HAD AN ASTROLOGICAL SIGN, IT WOULD BE: Scorpio.

ELEMENTS: Water, enchanted forests, mountains, shadows, dreamscape, imagination.

GEMSTONES WITH SIMILAR VIBRATION: Agate, amethyst, ametrine, aquamarine, aventurine (blue, green), crystal quartz, emerald, lapis lazuli, sugilite, turquoise.

FAVORITE SEASON(S): Fall and winter.

ANIMAL TOTEM(S): All aquatic life, deer, dolphins, white doves, rabbits, snakes, whales, wolves.

WING COLOR: White, but rarely shows them.

FAVORITE ATTIRE: White robe and a walking staff for the big and tall.

FAVORITE COLOR(S): Purple, turquoise, burgundy, black, silver.

FAVORITE FOOD(S): Tea is fine, thank you.

FAVORITE MUSIC: Flute and harp, tribal drums, Celtic.

IDEAL DATE: A quiet, moonlit evening sitting on the hill, watching a village below.

ASCENDED MASTERS AND BENEVOLENT SPIRIT TEACHERS WITH SIMILAR ENERGY SIGNATURES: Ishtar, Isis, Merlin, Neptune, St. Padre Pio.

NOTABLE PEOPLE WITH SIMILAR VIBRATION: Orlando Bloom, Sigmund Freud, Louise Hay, George Lucas, Carolyn Myss, Emeril Lagasse, Jimmy Page, Keanu Reeves, Gene Roddenberry, Susan Sarandon, Takao Usui, Oprah Winfrey, Dr. Daniel Hale Williams, Robin Williams, Marianne Williamson.

FAVORITE CONTEMPORARY FICTIONAL CHARACTERS: Gandalf, Yoda.

USUALLY ARRIVES IN YOUR LIFE: When healing or a significant transition is afoot.

RAPHAEL'S MANSION

When I walked into Raphael's mansion, I was quickly whisked away in imaginings of what Merlin's work room might look like. Gray castle walls with grand Gothic arches tower over a room that serves as both a library and an observatory. Everything that is mystical and fantastical can be found in Raphael's mansion, with its levitating plasma spheres, periodic lightning strikes across the vaulted ceiling, and an occasional unicorn making a soft landing on the balcony.

Tables are overrun with books, scrolls, jewels, and crystals. At the far end of the room is a spiral staircase that leads up to perhaps Raphael's greatest treasure, a telescope that would make poor Hubble blush. Not only is Raphael's telescope made out of gilded gold, but it dwarfs NASA's by about ten times. Comparing the Hubble to Raphael's contraption would be like comparing a Mini Cooper to a tank.

Orbiting the base of the golden telescope is a layout of planets, stars, and galaxies, all spinning and gyrating in universal harmony. The device even ticks like a clock, a crystal chime sounding on occasion. I stood there a moment, watching the base slowly spin, and couldn't help but chuckle as I thought of Raphael on his birthday some countless ages ago: "Gee, Dad! My very own telescope! Quick, grab the instructions and let's put it together!" I pictured a young Raphael eagerly tearing open a box heavy enough to sink Australia.

But just as spectacular as the interior of Raphael's mansion is the exterior. Seemingly locked in a perpetual dusk, with the sky in hues of deep red and purple, the lands are blanketed with forests and valleys against dark, mysterious mountains that belch fireballs every now and then. Down below, beneath the veil of trees, teems life of the fantastical kind: winged unicorns, miniature angels (you might know them better as fairy folk), and baby dragons. It's like a wildlife reserve for magical creatures, and Raphael oversees it all with his keen sight and his love for the imagination and all it can conjure.

> *The souls of those who don't have "cure" written*
> *in their life script are still made whole*
> *by Raphael's healing touch.*
> —Archangel Sandalphon

RAPHAEL MANIFEST

Raphael is truly a gentle giant. When he came into my life during a serious health crisis, he whispered soothing words of healing and placed his hands over my eyes to ease the pain of ceaseless weeping from depression. I had been sobbing for hours that night, but his presence eased my fears and his deep, soft voice eased my discontent.

When I first beheld Raphael, I couldn't believe what my mind's eye saw. He stands much taller than his warrior brother Michael, and has broader, stronger shoulders than I have ever seen on any American football player. I would even say his build is bulkier than Michael, but Raphael's strength lies not in his muscles, but in his heart. His touch is tender, and when you look into his deep brown eyes, you cannot help but feel at ease.

When I see Raphael in the foreground of a client's consultation, I know that my client is seeking healing—whether physical, emotional, or spiritual. Raphael's stance will tell me whether the client is willing to be healed or not; many of us will ask for healing but for one reason or another resist it. We could be used to illness, so used to it that we're complacent. Or we could resist healing because deep down inside, our doubts seem safer than our faith. If we doubt, we feel more at peace—there can be no disappointment. If we place our energy behind our faith, we might fear that disappointment can shake our beliefs. The what-ifs always haunt us, but Raphael's presence is there to thwart those feelings, to eliminate those doubts so that we can see not only the gift in our healing but the gifts in our illnesses, too.

I've often told people, "Metaphysically speaking, there is an inherent difference between being cured and being healed." You can certainly be one without the other. Being cured means you've eliminated the malady even if the causes of that malady are still near. Being healed strengthens your mind, your soul, and your heart. It opens your eyes to causes of the *dis-ease* so you can either avoid or eliminate them altogether. You may not be cured while being healed, but a healing also helps you to better understand why you are ill in the first place. It is this understanding that envelops the heart with peace, regardless of the outcome of a situation.

And that's the crux of it, isn't it? The issue of the outcome. As I teach students in my Reiki class, no one should go into a Reiki session seeking a specific result. This comes back to the idea of surrender. (When working with the angels, you can expect to encounter this idea often.) That is to say, I never approach a Reiki client with the mission of healing or curing any specific ailment. Just because a client comes to me with migraines doesn't mean I'm going to administer Reiki to the head only. No, in Reiki the practitioner is simply a conduit of love and God's healing energy. The energy knows where it needs to be, and it is up to God and the client's life script as to whether or not they will find reprieve that day—it is not up to me, or the client, or even the doctors.

As the patron of all healers, Raphael teaches us about surrender—"let go and let God"—not only when it comes to seeking healing in our bodies, but also in relation to seeking healing in our lives. Raphael is the gentle, guiding force that leads us to the understanding that true healers can take poisons and turn them into medicines. He brings us to the wisdom that within the worst of illnesses or the worst adversities lie beautiful gifts of love, charity, and compassion. If we strive to seek these out in all areas of our life afflicted with *dis-ease*, we will ultimately be healed of fear, anger, and regret. Eliminate these afflictions of the heart and soul, and who can say that the body won't follow?

> *If life isn't about human beings and living in harmony,*
> *then I don't know what it's about.*
> —ORLANDO BLOOM

ARCHANGEL

IOPHIEL

A NURTURER

Not even blind men can deny the beauty that is Iophiel.

—ARCHANGEL RAPHAEL

———+———

MEANING OF NAME: Beauty of God.

TRIVIA: Don't let her looks fool you. Like Michael, Iophiel is a fierce warrior angel. She can kick demonic butt without smearing her makeup or tousling her hair.

MESSAGE TO THE CONTEMPORARY WORLD: The illusion of beauty is pain.

PATRON ANGEL (TRADITIONALLY) OF: Painters, sculptors, masons, architects, visionaries, gardeners, artists in general, secrets.

PATRON ANGEL (CURRENTLY) OF: The above, plus art historians, art teachers, photographers, fashion designers and models, interior decorators, wedding planners, film directors and production crews, community beautification groups, art museum curators and benefactors, philanthropists.

RULER OF: Friday (Venus); co-rules with Sandalphon.

HEAVENLY ASSIGNMENT: Iophiel opens our eyes to the beauty of God that surrounds us, as well as to the beauty that dwells within the human soul.

DEMEANOR WHEN ON THE JOB: Iophiel always wears a smile. She is quick to offer encouragement to those with low self-esteem and inspiration to those in an artistic rut.

DEMEANOR WHEN AT PLAY: Iophiel is always at play and enjoys her work assisting those who are passionate about the creative process. Whether you're creating the next great masterpiece or re-creating yourself with a make-over, Iophiel only asks that you make the process enjoyable.

HUMAN ACCOMPLISHMENTS MOST PROUD OF: The phonograph and the cinema.

BACK IN THE DAY, SHE LIKED: Pageants and festivals that celebrate a culture's beauty. Carnival!

TODAY, SHE ENJOYS: The same (though people need to be reminded that Carnival is a celebration of life and not a competition in bra-cup sizes).

PET PEEVES: Beauty competitions of any kind ("the driving force behind many of them is anything but beautiful"); the growing obsession with cosmetic surgery; the growing preference for a computer rather than a paint brush or a hammer and chisel.

HOPE FOR THE WORLD (SERIOUS): For it to learn to appreciate natural beauty and stop worshipping the illusion of beauty.

HOPE FOR THE WORLD (WHIMSICAL): For it to not let banks dictate holidays. Make *every day* a celebration of love, friendship, and unity.

IF SHE HAD AN ASTROLOGICAL SIGN, IT WOULD BE: Cancer/Leo cusp.

ELEMENTS: Flowers, birds, rainbows, sunlight.

GEMSTONES WITH SIMILAR VIBRATION: Agate, chrysoprase, crystal quartz, Jade (green, pink), malachite, opal, rhodochrosite, rhodonite, rose quartz, ruby, tourmaline (green, pink).

FAVORITE SEASON(S): Spring and summer.

ANIMAL TOTEM(S): Peacock, swan.

WING COLOR: Pearl white.

FAVORITE ATTIRE: Robes of pastel colors, usually pink or green. During battle, she dons armor and white robes.

FAVORITE COLOR(S): All colors.

FAVORITE FOOD(S): Angel food cake … and devil's food cake. (She said this with quite an impish grin.)

FAVORITE MUSIC: Folk, the livelier the better. Big Band.

IDEAL DATE: Grape stomping contest, followed by a family feast and dancing.

ASCENDED MASTERS AND BENEVOLENT SPIRIT TEACHERS WITH SIMILAR ENERGY SIGNATURES: Aphrodite, Athena, Guinevere, Lakshmi, Mary Magdalene, Oonagh, Oshun, Vesta.

NOTABLE PEOPLE WITH SIMILAR VIBRATION: Drew Barrymore, Halle Berry, William Blake, RuPaul Andre Charles, Anne Geddes, Elton John, Janis Joplin, Milla Jovovich, Jackie Kennedy, Paul Newman, Maxfield Parrish, Queen Latifa, Abbott Handerson Thayer, Vanessa Williams, Catherine Zeta-Jones, Ziyi Zhang.

FAVORITE CONTEMPORARY FICTIONAL CHARACTERS: The Ugly Duckling, Clarence Oddbody (*It's a Wonderful Life*), Ren McCormack (*Footloose*), Mushu (*Mulan*), Ugly Betty.

USUALLY ARRIVES IN YOUR LIFE: When you need to slow down and make rest, respite, and recreation integral parts of the healing process, whether this is healing of the body, mind, or soul.

IOPHIEL'S MANSION

Color and culture! Iophiel's mansion is locked in a never-ending celebration of life and diversity.

I never know what I'm going to find when I step into this archangel's world. At one point it was a Tuscany villa against the backdrop of a sun-kissed vineyard. Another time I stepped into a celebration of Cinco de Mayo. Another time, when Sandalphon was visiting, there was a Mardi Gras–type festival equipped with lively jazz music, vibrant costumes, and dazzling parade floats.

Even if Iophiel wasn't home, someone else always was. There were always souls bustling about—an artist painting his next masterpiece, a mime on a street corner, village "locals" going about their daily business of food and festivities. There's a sense of joy and community in Iophiel's mansion. It's a place where everyone is welcome, the food is plentiful and the music and laughter never end.

So far, Iophiel's is the only angelic mansion in which I've actually witnessed human activity. That's not to say that humans don't appear elsewhere, but this was the only place where I've seen the souls take on recognizable human form. Usually, or as far as I've been shown, everyone on the other side is in spirit form.

I guess it's hard to eat red beans and rice or a po' boy if you've got no hands, though.

> *'Tis best to tango with Iophiel than tangle with her.*
> *Adversaries learn this the hard way.*
> —Archangel Michael

IOPHIEL MANIFEST

While interviewing Iophiel, I realized that not only was she an angel of beauty, but she was a beautiful angel. Her demeanor was so upbeat and cheerful that I couldn't help but be uplifted while listening to her chatter about the perfect devil's food cake. She was certainly not an advocate of dieting or portion control. Why should she be? She can eat whatever she wants and not gain a single pound.

"We humans have to be a bit more careful, I think," I said, chuckling as I wrote down my notes. I heard Iophiel sigh.

"Life doesn't have to be so structured all the time," she said softly.

Iophiel comes into our lives when we need shaking up in a good way, when we need to turn our sour frowns into smiles and open our hearts to love, compassion, and hope. True, the world may seem bleak, but she says it's only that way because that's what we wish to see. "Blame yourselves for that one," she told me as she unfolded her wings and shook out her hair.

I don't want in any way to trivialize an archangel, but she truly does remind me of a life-size Tinkerbell with a larger-than-life attitude. She went on to say that if we only purchase newspapers during tragedies or we keep clicking hyperlinks to stories about hate and war, then we continue to propagate it.

"But then again, Chantel, when was the last time you ever clicked on a good-news article?" she asked. Average American that I am, I'll admit to clicking on the more shocking or compelling stories, but after a while my soul will rebel and let me know when I've digested too much negativity. I do go out of my way to look for good news around the world and, thanks to the Internet, there are several reputable sites that focus on good news. They're struggling along, but they seem steadfast in their conviction to show a side of the world that mainstream media turns a blind eye to—the world of hope.

Iophiel approves of them. "It's a difficult mission, but they have my blessing. They are sorely needed in this age."

Iophiel was quick to change the topic, and her eyes really lit up when she started talking about festivals and pageants. Seems that those are her favorite pastimes, but I couldn't help but ask more about her grape-stomping comment in the interview.

"It's all about teamwork and having fun. Gabriel is a great swabbie! I, of course, prefer stomping. I've challenged Michael to a stomp or two and he hasn't taken me up on my offer. He can lead angelic armies from one universe to another, but seems to get squeamish when it comes to grapes." If I didn't know better, I could have sworn Iophiel was challenging her brother to a smackdown right there in my living room.

All play aside, Iophiel challenges us to embrace life with both arms and make the absolute best of what God gives us. She teaches us that compassion must begin with the self before it can branch out to others, and that we must be willing to acknowledge that everyone possesses within themselves the Spirit of God. Regardless of a person's culture, language, tradi-

tions, nationality, or religion, at their very core still resides the essence of God—and that is the core of our beauty.

"The problem," Iophiel said, "is that people often turn a blind eye either to the beauty within themselves or to the beauty in others. Seek the beauty in all that is around you and I promise that you will find it."

As you continue to read this book, you'll notice that Iophiel is the only archangel who took a female form when I interviewed her. I was stunned to find out, later, that she is traditionally considered a "he." As I've said before, angels will come to us in forms we are comfortable with. If anything, Iophiel showing up as female, when all the other archangels came to me as male, says more about me than anything else. I can't help it if I feel more comfortable discussing devil's food recipes with a girlfriend rather than a guy friend!

> *Imagination is the real and eternal world*
> *of which this vegetable universe is but a faint shadow.*
> —WILLIAM BLAKE

ARCHANGEL
MICHAEL

A WARRIOR

If you find yourself in the midst of a battle,
keep your eyes fixed on the adversary, your mind focused on your
objectives, and know that I have your back.

—ARCHANGEL MICHAEL

———+———

MEANING OF NAME: Who is as God.

TRIVIA: Michael is the Prince or Chief of the archangels. According to biblical texts, he ousted Lucifer during the Great War in Heaven.

MESSAGE TO THE CONTEMPORARY WORLD: Learn to laugh and approach life with childlike zeal.

PATRON ANGEL (TRADITIONALLY) OF: Police, firefighters, soldiers, protectors of truth and justice.

PATRON ANGEL (CURRENTLY) OF: The above, plus surfer dudes and dudettes, dancers, car racers, wrestlers, body builders, football players, basketball players, sun and beach worshippers, sports! sports! sports!

RULER OF: Sunday (Sun).

HEAVENLY ASSIGNMENT: The General of Heaven's armies and the most beloved angel.

DEMEANOR WHEN ON THE JOB: Michael is also the Universal Champion of Wrestling. He's the Terminator of the Universe, kicking demonic butt and taking names across the galaxies.

DEMEANOR WHEN AT PLAY: Playful, competitive, and light-hearted. He takes everything in stride.

HUMAN ACCOMPLISHMENTS MOST PROUD OF: Fire, the sword, the chariot, the phonograph, the automobile, space exploration.

BACK IN THE DAY, HE USED TO LIKE: Gladiators. "It was bloody, but hey, that's entertainment, folks."

TODAY, HE ENJOYS: The Super Bowl and the World Cup.

PET PEEVE: Believe it or not, war.

HOPE FOR THE WORLD (SERIOUS): For it to be at peace with itself and its role in God's Great Equation.

HOPE FOR THE WORLD (WHIMSICAL): For it to make more field goals and fewer weapons of mass destruction.

IF HE HAD AN ASTROLOGICAL SIGN, IT WOULD BE: Leo.

ELEMENTS: Fire, the beach, candles, sunlight, light, heat, energy (hates fluorescent lighting).

GEMSTONES WITH SIMILAR VIBRATION: Agate, bloodstone, carnelian, crystal quartz, diamond, garnet, hawk's eye.

FAVORITE SEASON(S): Summer.

ANIMAL TOTEM(S): Bears, eagles, falcons, hawks, lions (likes the sports teams, too).

WING COLOR: White.

FAVORITE ATTIRE: Typical white angel robe, minus the sleeves (or the tunic entirely) to show off the muscles and instill fear into anyone stupid enough to provoke him.

FAVORITE COLOR(S): Gold, orange, yellow.

FAVORITE FOOD(S): Spicy Mexican and Thai.

FAVORITE MUSIC: Blues, Rock & Roll, Hip Hop, Reggae, Funk.

IDEAL DATE: Sunbathing on the beach, followed by a picnic, volleyball, and a marshmallow toast.

ASCENDED MASTERS AND BENEVOLENT SPIRIT TEACHERS WITH SIMILAR ENERGY SIGNATURES: Apollo, Brigit, Horus, Krishna, Kuan Ti, Odin, Pelé.

NOTABLE PEOPLE WITH SIMILAR VIBRATION: Muhammad Ali, Jennifer Aniston, Lance Armstrong, Fred Astaire, Tyra Banks, Sean Connery, Paula Dean, Clint Eastwood, Laurence Fishburne, Michael Jackson, Samuel L. Jackson, Heath Ledger, Madonna, Barry Manilow, Marilyn Monroe, Brad Pitt, Princess Diana of Wales, Britney Spears, Barbra Streisand,

Charlize Theron, Justin Timberlake, Steven Tyler, John Wayne, Reese Witherspoon, Tiger Woods, Jay Z.

FAVORITE CONTEMPORARY FICTIONAL CHARACTERS: Bugs Bunny, Captain Jack Sparrow, Cheshire Cat, Rocky and Bullwinkle, Teenage Mutant Ninja Turtles, all super heroes from both Marvel and DC Comics.

USUALLY ARRIVES IN YOUR LIFE: When the environment in which you live is about to drastically change, whether due to a new residence, a new job/career, or a change in family/friend dynamics.

michael's mansion

As with all the other angel mansions, I've visited Michael's several times. To say the least, the Prince of Angels is quite a showman, and it's evident by the sheer size of the mansion alone.

Michael's mansion is one of the largest of the twelve, and calling it a mansion is a gross understatement. It's more like an estate the size of China, where the land is plush and green and wild horses run free. Rolling, sun-crested hills provide a stunning backdrop to the main palace, eight football fields long and wide, that carefully blends ancient Egyptian and Roman architecture.

In the courtyard, three statues of charging war horses tower overhead, protecting the entrance of the palace. The look in their eyes is menacing. Their thick, muscled legs rear with hooves high in the air, and their wild manes seem frozen in time, caught in a moment of triumph and glory. As I tiptoed past the statues on my first visit, their eyes followed me, brows furrowed in suspicion. I would hate to see what would happen if anyone of ill intent stumbled upon this trio.

Inside the foyer, I was welcomed by elaborate Egyptian paintings of chariot races and warriors that seemed to leap off the sandstone walls, but in the center of the foyer—as if the sentinel horses weren't enough warning—levitated a two-handed greatsword of steel. Its hilt was detailed in gold, and the blade was lighted with wild wisps of flames, pointed skyward.

Further into the palace—well, as far as I was willing to venture inside the behemoth—stood Egyptian sarcophagi against grand sandstone columns, which added to the feeling that I was exploring an ancient tomb rather than an angel's mansion. But I was soon reminded of where I was when I entered one of the great halls (the stone pillars made the room look like a giant chess board). On one side were statues representing the Egyptian Empire—pharaohs, their royal courts, and obelisks holding up a ceiling that spans stories-high overhead. On the other side was the Roman Empire. While the figures all stood like skyscrapers supporting a ceiling painted with stars, planets, and galaxies, their pawns were hunched low, foot soldiers

all wielding their weapon of choice—from the bow and arrow, to the sword, to the javelin.

For the most part, the palace was full of sunlight, but there were darker little alcoves and such that held interesting treasures: papyrus scrolls, suits of armor, and more statues and weapons—lots and lots of weapons, from the Neolithic Age right up through the Middle Ages.

I could have stopped after the first mile or so of walking. Honestly, I'm not sure how far I walked, but when your feet begin to hurt in a meditation and you begin to feel winded, it's a sign to pull back for a while. But before I left, something drew me in just a bit further, through two monstrous doors gilded with burnished gold and onto a mezzanine. There I beheld one of the largest and most elaborate swimming pools I've ever seen. Its size equaled about six Olympic-sized pools; it was more like an indoor lake.

The deck of the pool was a mosaic of black, silver, and gold tiles, all reflecting the amber glow of the lighted torches on the walls. A heavy scent of sandalwood filled the air. But the most interesting part about the pool was its dark, rippling waters. It's a wave pool, with waters so dense in color that it doesn't give up the mystery of how deep it is, or what lurks beneath.

I spotted another set of doors, clear at the other end of the room, that were silver in color and embossed with two robust falcon profiles.

My feet couldn't get me down the stairs to the pool deck fast enough. Then I heard, "Tour's over."

"Aw, c'mon, Michael. Show me, I wanna see!" It's that type of curiosity that gets people into a lot of trouble, I know. Let's not forget what happened to Lot's wife when she just had to look back at the destruction of Sodom and Gomorrah. Somewhere in a diner, what's left of her is sitting at a table-for-two in a salt shaker.

Regardless, I was still pulled toward those massive silver doors. After all, one was just slightly open as if inviting me inside. Despite Michael's first warning, I continued alongside that pool of dark, eerie water toward the doors. Then it seemed that Michael turned up the heat on the wall torches a bit, sending flames high over my head. I stopped in my tracks, and then made a speedy about-face.

"All righty then, it's been nice, Prince." With a swift genuflect, I scampered back up to the mezzanine and out of the meditation. What lies behind those doors, I haven't a clue. Naturally, because I wasn't allowed a peek, my inquisitiveness is higher than ever. Would whatever I discover behind the doors be too much for my human mind to comprehend or process? Would passing through the forbidden doors end the world as we know it? All right, so the notion is a bit melodramatic. Still, I cannot help but imagine Michael lounging behind those doors on an ornate dais, dressed in an outfit that would make Egyptian pharaohs jealous and the gods blush. Yes, I can picture gold vambraces on his arms and cuffs hugging his massive, tawny biceps as he sits there looking more like a god of the sun than a son of God. Could it be that he didn't want me to catch him playing dress-up? Hey, a girl can dream, right?

I have plans to wear Michael down and see if he'll be willing to give me a backstage tour one day. I'll be sure to keep you posted—if I make it out alive, without being attacked by one of the mummies or any flesh-eating scarabs.

> *I've handled the biggest and best of wars against Light's most formidable enemies, so I think I can handle your nagging boss and that snobby clerk at that trendy coffee shop. No, I don't need your input either. Just consider me your auto-pilot, let go of the controls, and enjoy your flight.*
> —ARCHANGEL MICHAEL

MICHAEL MANIFEST

When Michael comes to the fore in our lives, it is to bolster our courage and confidence when external changes in our environment are about to take place. He illuminates the darkness of uncharted territory with his golden light, helping to dispel our fears of the Unknown and the uncertain, and he teaches us to focus on our own God-given gifts and skills to help carry us through times of tumult.

Michael teaches us to be warriors in life and to be on the constant lookout for our mortal enemy—ourselves. But beware, the same ego that feeds our arrogance and greed is also the ego that feeds our low self-esteem and self-loathing. This is the demon that we must overcome. The devil that comes to undo us works not beneath our feet in a pit of fire, but resides in our very souls to turn us toward anger, hate, pride, greed, dissension, and conflict. Michael teaches us to guard ourselves against these afflictions of the soul, for the only adversary that this archangel cannot protect us from is ourselves. Still, Michael helps keep us in check by sending us signs of eagles, birds of prey, lions, swords, sunlight, or fire to let us know he is forever present in our lives. Whether you're in prayer, meditation, or standing at life's crossroads, these signs are Michael's way of letting you know, "Hey, I got your back."

Let Michael worry about the external demons and devils of the universe. You just focus on the shadows within yourself and defeat them by bringing the light of love and wisdom to the fore of your life. If you walk into the darkness, there is no way you can combat it, manipulate it, or tell it to go away. The only way to dissipate darkness is to bring light to it; Michael, in all his radiant splendor, has plenty to share with the entire cosmos. All you need do is ask, and he will more than happily shine your way.

One quality that is often overlooked in Michael, however, is his playfulness. Michael loves to laugh, and even loves playing harmless pranks on his archangel brothers (especially Gabriel). He is a bright and jovial spirit with a contagious laugh that can soothe the soul and force a smile to the lips of the sourest miser. His heart is golden, his face is pure light, and the will of God radiates through him. There is nothing in this universe that does not recognize Michael's strength and majesty, nor do his sunny personality and love of sports go unnoticed.

> *The sun, with all those planets revolving around it*
> *and dependent on it, can still ripen a bunch of grapes*
> *as if it had nothing else in the universe to do.*
> —GALILEO GALILEI

ARCHANGEL

URIEL

A WARRIOR

I've seen Uriel smile ... once.

—ARCHANGEL CASSIEL

———+———

MEANING OF NAME: Fire of God.

TRIVIA: According to biblical accounts, Uriel "escorted" Adam and Eve from the Garden of Eden.

MESSAGE TO THE CONTEMPORARY WORLD: Is the End here yet?

PATRON ANGEL (TRADITIONALLY) OF: Judges, lawmakers, peace-makers, seekers of truth, upholders of justice, prophets, visionaries.

PATRON ANGEL (CURRENTLY) OF: The same.

RULER OF: Tuesday (Mars).

HEAVENLY ASSIGNMENT: To bring humanity before the throne of God on the Day of Reckoning.

DEMEANOR WHEN ON THE JOB: Has a disdain for humanity in general and can't wait for Judgment Day to come.

DEMEANOR WHEN AT PLAY: Doesn't play.

HUMAN ACCOMPLISHMENTS MOST PROUD OF: Not interested.

BACK IN THE DAY, HE LIKED: Days before the Earth was created.

TODAY, HE ENJOYS: Countdown to when this "debacle" is over.

PET PEEVE: Humanity's tendency for greed, lies, deception, and pettiness.

HOPE FOR THE WORLD (SERIOUS): "I've hope only for a select few and they know who they are."

HOPE FOR THE WORLD (WHIMSICAL): *Author didn't even bother to ask Uriel.*

IF HE HAD AN ASTROLOGICAL SIGN, IT WOULD BE: Sagittarius

ELEMENTS: Fire and brimstone, void, volcanoes, earthquakes, lightning, thunder, floods.

GEMSTONES WITH SIMILAR VIBRATION: Agate, apache tears, crystal quartz, jet, obsidian.

FAVORITE SEASON(S): No preference.

ANIMAL TOTEM(S): Phoenix.

WING COLOR: Crimson and gold.

FAVORITE ATTIRE: Crimson armor with elaborate gold detailing.

FAVORITE COLOR(S): Red, gold.

FAVORITE FOOD(S): Barbecued anything.

FAVORITE MUSIC: "The dragging of chains used to capture the world's iniquitous inhabitants."

IDEAL DATE: Not interested.

ASCENDED MASTERS AND BENEVOLENT SPIRIT TEACHERS WITH SIMILAR ENERGY SIGNATURES: Forseti, Idaten, Lilith, Maat, Thor, Thoth.

NOTABLE PEOPLE WITH SIMILAR VIBRATION: Aristotle, Socrates.

FAVORITE CONTEMPORARY FICTIONAL CHARACTERS: Godzilla, Darth Vader, Agent Smith of *The Matrix*, Magneto of *X-Men*.

USUALLY ARRIVES IN YOUR LIFE: I have rarely seen Uriel in consultations. In ten years, I can probably count on one hand my encounters with him, and those encounters were deeply serious in nature, usually involving someone's path as a scholar or prophet.

uriel's mansion

Warm and fuzzy is not something that ever comes to mind when thinking of Uriel. As one of heaven's resident cynics and an angel who has something of a disdain for humanity as a whole, Uriel has chosen a motif for his mansion that is hardly welcoming. If anything, I think he has Michael topped as far as the "do not enter" hints at his mansion's entrance. That's not to say that Uriel doesn't have style. If I may be so bold as to express my personal tastes regarding his mansion, I think it is *wicked cool*.

A grand palace like Michael's, Uriel's mansion is hardly basking in sunlight or surrounded by rolling green hills. It sits atop a towering dark mountain; rivers of molten lava flow slowly downhill into a dismal landscape. As I stood at the top of the mountain and looked out into the infinity of a nighttime lighted only by flames, I felt as if I were the only person alive. I hoped to fare better once I got inside.

I have a deep trust and adoration for Uriel, even in all his stoic mannerisms, and so I felt no fear as I ventured into his lair. Entering the foyer, I was met with fire-filled cauldrons that illuminated halls painted in crimson and detailed in gold. In the great hall, red silk banners wave between pillars that touch the starless sky. All was eerily quiet. There are no paintings, statues, or anything of human cultural influence. It's almost as if Uriel went out of his way to not remind himself of those pesky bipedal mammals on Earth. Yet there is armor: breastplates, shields, weapons, and a single chariot that sits in the main hall. While compared to Michael's mansion this one is stark, it is not without its own exotic beauty. There is something to be said about the drapes of silk that hang about; Uriel can be menacing, but it seems that he has an elegant side to him as well.

I ventured farther through the mansion and came to a room that actually looked lived-in, with chairs and divans made of aged cherry wood. Swords adorn the walls here, swords with nicks, scratches, even scorching, swords that have seen plenty of battle. Whether they were Uriel's or trophies garnished from the vanquished I wasn't sure, but each sword tells a tale of fierce combat between two unrelenting foes. Toward the back the room, dark, wooden shelves stocked with books line the wall and flank a set of double doors made of a substance that shines like the volcanic glass obsidian. Well, the last pair of ominous double doors I saw were in Michael's mansion, and I got booted from there before I could open them. I put my hands on the handles and looked up, waiting for a warning from Uriel.

When I heard no such warning, I gave both doors a hearty pull and come face to face with two giant Chinese dragons. They looked at me. I looked at them. I screamed. They roared and shook the entire room. I was just about to run in the opposite direction when I saw they were chained at the collar, like guard dogs.

"Well, you two don't ... look that scary." I calmed myself down and beheld the creatures—one black and one red with a gold shimmer to their scales. My words weren't cold before Red made himself known as a living napalm tank. It was just then that I had a flash of a memory, a dream from decades prior about two great dragons. So I retaliated with my own hot air.

"Red, cut it out!" I screamed, and the flames stopped abruptly. Both dragons looked at me, stupefied. "You both know better," I growled, stomping toward them. Both of them backed up, the wusses. Well, not really. I'm sure someone else would have ended up a charcoal briquette, but I knew both flame-throwers and they knew me, thankfully. Red is actually like a giant lapdog who loves to play, while Black sits and broods like his father, Uriel. I sat with the two a while—dragon-sitting, as it were—until lo and behold, Uriel showed up.

"Having fun?" The fiery angel leaned against the doorframe and crossed his arms, his piercing eyes leveled on me.

"Yeap, just wish I had marshmallows." I chuckled as Red's tail wagged like a puppy.

"You'll find those at Sandalphon's." Uriel shook his head and walked away with long, purposeful strides and a straight back, as if he were ready for battle at the drop of a hat.

"Uriel, wait!" I scrambled after the angel, narrowly missing Red's playful attempts to grab me and drag me back.

Uriel stopped in midstride, turning his head just slightly to glance at me over his shoulder. "Can I help you, little one?" He lips barely moved, seemingly locked into a thin, grim line. Then he headed up a spiral staircase, into a turret full of—you guessed it—weapons.

"Yes. I'd like an interview," I managed to say as I followed him into the turret.

"Must I?" He sighed and slung a quiver of arrows over his shoulder. I gazed in awe at the medieval arsenal before me, and went to touch one of the more menacing looking swords—a serrated broadsword with deep, curving teeth that could gut and filet an enemy in two moves.

"Don't touch that," Uriel warned, his back to me. I quickly withdrew my hand and stuck it in my pocket. "Michael sent you, didn't he?"

"No, but he got a royal kick out of the fact you're on my list of angels to interview."

Uriel mumbled something faint but it sounded like, *Heaven may very well lose its General tonight*. "How long will this ... interview take?"

"Thirty minutes?" I tried giving him a beguiling smile.

His eyebrows knit together over those blazing green eyes.

"How about twenty?"

He shifted his weight to one foot, his hands clutching the strap of his quiver so tightly his knuckles were as white as chalk. Still, I've never been one to give in.

"Geeze, you're an angel! I thought time meant nothing to you guys. I'm the one with the deadline here!"

Uriel's answering growl could have made a lion cower.

"Fine. Fifteen minutes?" I folded my arms and mimicked his obstinate stance and stoic gaze.

"How about none?" He stormed toward me, took my hand, and slapped a slip of parchment into my palm. "Close the door when you leave." And he was gone.

I unfolded the parchment to find his answers to my interview questions. Well, to most of them. "You know," I yelled over my shoulder at the door, "I'm sure Raphael could help you with your anti-social issues! There are medications for that these days."

Lightning flashed outside the window, and thunder shook the tower.

"Love you too, Uri."

> *If Uriel was put in charge of death,*
> *we angels would be unemployed.*
> —ARCHANGEL MICHAEL

URIEL MANIFEST

Because I usually research and write about angels or ascended masters *after* they've established a connection with me, I had very little to say about Uriel in the beginning. I had met this quiet (but sharp-tongued-when-provoked) archangel years ago, but our exchanges were brief at best. Whenever I engaged in casual group chat with Michael, Raphael, and Gabriel ("the boys," as my clients have dubbed them), Uriel would lurk in the distance, a silent sentinel who had little to offer to casual conversation. Originally, even his appearance mimicked his remoteness: elfin—for easy hiding—with obscure features. I never got a full view of Uriel's countenance even on the rare occasion when we spoke face to face. It was as if he were in a video where his face was blurred to hide his identity; Uriel was one of the most mysterious angels I had yet met.

It was only when I made the conscious decision to understand my future as an angel medium that Uriel made himself fully known to me. The fiery angel of prophecy, metaphysics, and universal balance transformed his appearance and came to me, that day in his mansion, as a towering, chiseled-faced red-head with a deep and commanding voice that could shake mountains with the slightest whisper. He is fiercely beautiful— "fierce" being the emphasis here.

Uriel's well-publicized discontent with humanity only fuels his reputation as an Angel of Retribution. He has command of fire, lightning, thunder, and earthquakes, and according to biblical lore, he is the angel who will bring God's wrath upon the ever-iniquitous human race. He is also said to have the job of bringing humans and demons alike before the throne of God for the final judgment. And based on what I've personally seen of Uriel's angst, I think this archangel can't wait for that day to come.

But fire and brimstone aside, Uriel's role in our lives is to bestow wisdom and understanding. He helps us identify self-destructive behaviors that undermine our spiritual growth.

Let thine heart retain my words: keep my commandments, and live. Get wisdom, get understanding: forget it not, neither decline from the words of my mouth. Forsake [wisdom] not, and she shall preserve thee; love her, and she shall keep thee. Wisdom is the principal thing; therefore get wisdom: and with all thy getting get understanding. Exalt her, and she shall promote thee; she shall bring thee to honour, when thou dost embrace her. She shall give to thine head an ornament of grace: a crown of glory shall she deliver to thee.

PROVERBS 4:4–9

Uriel is the enforcer of this philosophy. He demands that those under his watch live with honor and speak and act in perfect knowledge. He blesses those who strive to walk this path with the gifts of prophecy and mysticism.

These gifts, however, do not come without a heavy price, since Uriel is also the Archangel of Consciousness and is forever whispering guidance into the ears of those he protects (some of my clients prefer to call it "guilt" rather than "guidance"). He is that "little angel" on your shoulder telling you to inform the kid at the drive-thru window that he gave you too much change, testing your integrity and your ability to be honest 100 percent of the time, not just when someone's watching. You know that nagging guilt you feel after an argument in which you *knew* you were wrong but wanted the last word anyhow? Uriel. That pinch of reality when the tables turn and others do unto you after you have unjustly done unto them? Uriel. While I'd like to hold on to the hope that everyone reading this book can breathe a sigh of relief and say, "I've been an angel all my life," both my skepticism and Uriel say "*riiiiiight*." Don't get me wrong; I'm in no position to cast the first stone myself. That's another book all its own. As I tell everyone, "I walk and talk with the angels—but alas, an angel I am not."

Uriel serves as a constant reminder to beware of spiritual snares like anger and fear, and helps to keep us on the straight and narrow. He also helps us conquer our own egos. All of us fall victim to our egos—be it issues of control, pride, or vanity, just to name a few—and Uriel enables us to push past these pitfalls by helping us recognize our spiritual identity. By recognizing our spiritual selves, we can better recognize, relate to, and connect to the spiritual identity of others. We are forced to be honest with ourselves and others, revealing our underlying, ego-based obstacles so that we may face and conquer them. In essence, Uriel is the mirror of truth into which we must gaze if we are to engage in any form of spiritual elevation.

But these pitfalls ... can one conquer them completely? Permanently?

The answer is "yes." Of course, it is a lifelong practice and the results can take years to surface. Because such transitions are gradual and often attained through much trial and error, Uriel becomes the literal fire under our tails that gets us moving along this journey. He helps us to take the first steps, or tows us out of a spiritual rut somewhere down the road.

Because he is painfully intense and takes his role as The Fire of God seriously, you better have a darn good reason to call on Uriel. He is not the "help me find my car keys" angel. Uriel appreciates deep, reflective conversation and encourages those under his watch to pattern their lives accordingly. They must avoid pettiness and avoid getting caught up in the whirlwinds of social climates and status quo—or anything that draws attention away from spiritual growth.

I would never be so foolish as to take Uriel lightly, but I rather enjoy his cynicism, as it sometimes matches my own angst about the world. So if you are moved by injustice, angered by humanity's seeming inability to cultivate a harmonious relationship with itself, I suggest you talk to Uriel. Allow him to reveal the issues *you* must first overcome in order to be best equipped to help others do likewise. In doing this, we can beautify our human tapestry one soul at a time.

> *I count him braver who overcomes his desires*
> *than him who conquers his enemies;*
> *for the hardest victory is over self.*
> —ARISTOTLE

ARCHANGEL

CASSIEL

A WARRIOR

For every one tear you weep, I will weep thousands.

—Archangel Cassiel

———+———

Meaning of name: Speed of God.

Trivia: Cassiel is sometimes considered the Angel of Karma or Retribution (vengeance), since he rules over Saturn, which represents karma.

Message to the contemporary world: The rules have not changed. "For with what judgment ye judge, ye shall be judged: and with what measure ye mete, it shall be measured to you again." Matthew 7:2

Patron angel (traditionally) of: The oppressed, the downtrodden, the impoverished, the enslaved, the unjustly persecuted, orphaned children.

Patron angel (currently) of: The same.

Ruler of: Saturday (Saturn); co-rules with Azrael.

HEAVENLY ASSIGNMENT: Known as the Angel of Tears, Cassiel offers his presence to those in need of comfort during their most sorrowful moments.

DEMEANOR WHEN ON THE JOB: Quiet, comforting.

DEMEANOR WHEN AT PLAY: "As long as there is strife, there will never be time to play."

HUMAN ACCOMPLISHMENTS MOST PROUD OF: Still waiting to be impressed.

BACK IN THE DAY, HE LIKED: Knights who fought with valor and honor.

TODAY, HE ENJOYS: Those who question and step outside the status quo.

PET PEEVES: The caste system; nepotism; cronyism.

HOPE FOR THE WORLD (SERIOUS): For it to find the unity between the mind, body, and soul.

HOPE FOR THE WORLD (WHIMSICAL): For it to understand that when random acts of kindness only happen on one state-appointed day, they're not so random. Making a conscious effort to practice acts of kindness on a regular basis would be so much more effective.

IF HE HAD AN ASTROLOGICAL SIGN, IT WOULD BE: Aquarius.

ELEMENTS: Rain, big cities, old church buildings, cemeteries, nighttime, moonlight, dreamscape.

GEMSTONES WITH SIMILAR VIBRATION: Agate, crystal quartz, hematite, jasper, kunzite, pyrite.

FAVORITE SEASON(S): Fall and winter.

ANIMAL TOTEM(S): Snow owl, raven, crow, dragon, koi.

WING COLOR: Dark gray to blue-black.

FAVORITE ATTIRE: Cloaks of navy or gray with tunics of burgundy (formal); black leather trench coat, tattered black denim, and biker boots (informal).

FAVORITE COLOR(S): Black.

FAVORITE FOOD(S): Thai, Chinese, Japanese, Indian.

FAVORITE MUSIC: Baroque, Hard Rock, Goth, Ambient, Techno.

IDEAL DATE: A moonlit night, preferably Halloween, sitting atop a bell tower and watching the clouds go by. Better yet, a trip through Saturn's rings—it's like bumper cars after three double espressos.

ASCENDED MASTERS AND BENEVOLENT SPIRIT TEACHERS WITH SIMILAR ENERGY SIGNATURES: An angelic chameleon of sorts, Cassiel's natural ability for adaptation to any environment and situation makes him a bit unpredictable, especially from a psychic's perspective. He accompanies all of Heaven's manifestations to lend a helping hand anywhere and everywhere he can.

NOTABLE PEOPLE WITH SIMILAR VIBRATION: Aaliyah, Susan B. Anthony, Ludwig van Beethoven, Johnny Cash, Jackie Chan, Dave Chapelle, Ray Charles, Russell Crowe, Johnny Depp, Houdini, Ice T, Angelina Jolie, Frida Kahlo, Bruce Lee, Bob Marley, Joseph Merrick, Jim Morrison, Willie Nelson, Gary Oldman, Rosa Parks, River Phoenix, Pablo Picasso, Edgar Allen Poe, Richard Pryor, Daniel Radcliffe, Anne Rice, Chris Rock, Oliver Stone, Harriet Tubman, Tina Turner.

FAVORITE CONTEMPORARY FICTIONAL CHARACTERS: Harry Potter, Batman, the Crow, Dr. Van Helsing and Dracula, Frankenstein, Quasimodo.

USUALLY ARRIVES IN YOUR LIFE: When you are at your darkest hour, feeling abandoned by all that you held dear. When your heart is heaviest and overflowing with tears, Cassiel appears to help shoulder the burdens of your woes and keep feelings of hopelessness at bay.

cassiel's mansion

Cassiel's mansion is an extraordinary and striking vision of Gothic architecture, with touches of feudal Japanese influence. The samurai suits of armor and weaponry seem a bit out of place in a mansion that looks more like a Catholic cathedral.

Unlike the other angelic mansions, Cassiel's is the only one that looks aged, with crumbling pillars and broken statues seemingly locked in perpetual mourning. The castle sits silently on barren grounds against the backdrop of a dark forest. Its walls are bathed in blue moonlight in an otherwise starless sky, and gruesome gargoyles guard the courtyard. Visitors are posed two choices: either brave the menacing creatures whose eyes follow your every move, or stand in the courtyard and freeze to death. Cassiel's mansion is the coldest of the twelve, with the thermostat locked at *late autumn*.

Moving into the foyer, I was welcomed by two altars containing hundreds of red votives, all lighted despite the strong drafts howling through the front corridor. The altars flank the main doors, which lead into a chapel. It was there that I beheld a sight that was both magical and solemn. Dusty pews sat empty and covered with cobwebs, but moonlight shone through the stained glass windows, each of which depicts an archangel in his best form: Michael wielding a sword of flames; Gabriel sounding his trumpet as he sits upon a rearing white stallion; purple flames dancing in the palms of Raphael's hands; Sandalphon's heart radiating with beams of sunlight; Chamuel holding his arms up, extending his staff to command the elements of nature; Uriel riding his chariot of fire with his chains in tow; Ramiel holding an open tome and a spinning hourglass; Iophiel posing with a quarterstaff of bright white light as rose blossoms flow from her robes; Raguel standing like a sentinel, his gaze alone enough to put the fear of God into an enemy; Metatron's light swirling in a cloud of brilliant colors; and Azrael wielding his scythe as he rides a horse's skeleton. There is one window that is bricked in—and by process of elimination, I knew it was Cassiel's.

He's so modest.

In the many rooms of Cassiel's mansion I found dark and foreboding libraries, storage for weaponry, or simply emptiness. Most of the rooms seemed unused, cold and unwelcoming. Bleak? Perhaps, but I didn't really expect much from an angel whose main purpose is to take on the sorrows of the world.

A highlight of his frigid abode, however—if you can even call it that—are his two pet black dragons who guard the castle's perimeter. They are stunning giants, just as graceful on the ground as they are in the air. I know Cassiel is very fond of them, and the only time I've ever really seen the archangel smile is when he spends time with them. I, on the other hand, prefer to keep a safe distance unless Cassiel is nearby. And to my surprise, I find him in his mansion quite often. It's not that he's loafing on the job. Remember, angels are multitaskers and can be in many places at once. But deep down inside, I think that while Cassiel is hard at work serving humankind as a refuge, he sometimes has to take refuge himself.

> *Three angels mysteriously go AWOL on Halloween:*
> *Michael's in it for the tricks. Sandalphon wants the treats.*
> *Cassiel just sits back and enjoys the fact that so many*
> *humans are dressed up like him.*
>
> —ARCHANGEL METATRON

CASSIEL MANIFEST

I'm going to take the liberty of saying that Archangel Cassiel is my personal favorite. He is probably the most cryptic and misunderstood angel in Heaven. Little is written on Cassiel, mainly because he is an observer at most and, according to religious texts, interacts little with humans. His position as an Angel of Solitude hasn't changed much, and his silence over the millennia has given seers and authors alike little to work with. But today Cassiel's workload has increased a bit, and he seems to have actually enjoyed assimilating with modern culture in order to better connect with humans of this age. Even with the assimilation, those who encounter Cassiel would probably mistake him for anything but an archangel, which is why I believe so little is said about him even in modern circles. He just doesn't fit the angel archetype—and I'm reminded of that every time he shows up in a consultation.

One of my most memorable moments with Cassiel was through a client that we'll call Sarah.

Sarah had come to the teashop one Sunday afternoon with a few of her friends for a Victorian-style high tea. Like the checkout counter, I had become a permanent fixture of the store and was relaxing out front with a cup of lavender mint, wondering if the owner was going to toss me an apron and ask me to help her out. Well, I didn't have to wear an apron that day, but I was asked to put on my intuition cap.

"Chantel, are you in the mood for a consultation today?" The owner stepped out on the sunlit porch to get a breather from the step-n-fetch routine that high teas often require.

"I'm always in the mood," I smirked back at her. I finished my tea, meandered inside, and tip-toed upstairs to prepare the meeting room.

Cassiel was already there.

Perched on the foot of the Reiki table like a stone-faced gargoyle gazing at a city skyline, he lifted his crystal-gray eyes to me from beneath a mess of jet-black hair.

"Well, hello stranger," I mused quietly. "How's Jake?" Because I was working more with Gabriel at the time, I hadn't seen Jake, my spirit guide, for quite a while and so felt the need to ask about him. After all, he had introduced me to Cassiel, his guardian angel, and I had been immediately taken by the angel's dark and mysterious demeanor.

"He's cool. Busy," Cassiel mumbled and returned his gaze to the floor. It was a distant gaze, as if he could see through the carpet, hardwood, and plaster right into the dining room below—where Sarah was still sitting.

"Aren't we all?" I lit a bowl of white sage. I could feel the heaviness of Cassiel's presence and understood that he was not an angel of idle chitchat, so I remained silent, sending my prayers of gratitude to the Heavens until Sarah came up.

Sarah entered the reading room with trepidation. It didn't take intuitive gifts to see that she was tense and unsure if she'd made the right decision in venturing up to see me. I introduced myself, explaining to her first and foremost what I was (an angel medium) and what I wasn't (a fortune-teller). It took a few seconds for the revelation to sink in, but when it did, Sarah leaned into the table and took a breath, as if to speak. Immediately, I held up my hand to stop her.

"Let the angels talk first, and *then* you can tell me why you're here." I closed my eyes and was immediately drawn into a vision of Cassiel, not standing beside Sarah, but perched high atop an old house. Thunder rumbled in the distance, but it was already gray, cold, and raining. Not helping to lighten the atmosphere, which was already desolate and bleak, was Cassiel's silence. Unlike all my other consultations, in which an angel conveys to me their course of action in a client's life, in this one Cassiel just sat, unmoving.

"Um, Cass, what are we waiting for?" I sat beside him, feeling the chill of the rain. He hushed me and I followed his piercing gaze across the street to another house, a rather large and expensive-looking Tudor with a horseshoe drive.

"Yeah. It's a house, Cass," I grumbled, urging him to quickly give me something to work with, and that's when I heard it: a thundering voice over the patter of the rain. It was a voice full of rage and blame, cursing and threatening. Then I heard another voice—smaller, meek and frightened. Lightning struck the house, startling me, but what scared me right out of the vision was the soul-curdling screams that followed.

"Tell her she can cry now. Tell her she's safe," Cassiel whispered. It was a message that I delivered while holding back my own tears. Sarah, who looked to be in her early forties, had suffered a lifelong pattern of abuse. Not only did she have to tiptoe around her mother, who was physically abusive, but she did all she could to avoid her father and older brothers, who were verbally abusive. And at a very young age, she had learned that crying was a sign of weakness, a weakness that her family preyed upon without mercy.

The fear of being preyed upon had followed Sarah into her adult years. Cassiel revealed to me how that fear had turned into anxiety and the compulsion to be in control of every area of her life. With my eyes closed and gazing at her spiritual form, I could see immediately the tension in her body, the stiffness in her neck, back and hips—all signs of unwillingness to yield or compromise—as well as what Cassiel called "a congestion of tears" in her heart center. As I relayed the information to her, I could feel her tension increase, much like a rubber band ready to snap.

"Sarah, do you need a break?" I offered as I opened my eyes. She was sitting, stiff-shouldered, with her hands balled up in white-knuckled fists on the table. She simply shook her head no.

"Crying is not a sign of weakness, Sarah," I whispered. "We all need that emotional release every now and then, men as well as women. Cassiel urges you to lean on his shoulder and not be afraid of being judged or criticized. He'll share your pain and your tears."

"I've never heard of Cassiel. What does he look like?" Sarah's voice was barely audible even in the silence of the room.

"Well..." I began and then stopped short. Though I had known Cassiel for the better part of a decade, I thought about just how different he looked from his archangel brothers. Also known as the Archangel of Tears and the Archangel of Restoration, he doesn't fit the Archangel archetype of white wings and a billowing white robe. He told me long ago, "I'm nothing like my brothers." To say the least, while he's not an angel of sunshine like Michael, he is an archangel nonetheless.

"Cass wouldn't wear white if his existence depended on it," Michael once told me, and in the time I've gotten to know this dark knight who rides upon the backs of dragons, the brightest color I've seen Cassiel yet wear is burgundy. Often donning a dark cloak, he loves working in the moonlight. With owls and ravens at his side, he comes to comfort those who have been unjustly persecuted. He opens his heart to our pain and helps us to feel not so alone in the world when all seems dark. With a determination to set the wrong things right, his message to us is, "I come not for you to believe in me, but for you to believe in yourself."

Sarah, looking a little disturbed when I told her she had a neo-Goth archangel on her shoulder, glanced warily up at the ceiling and then at both her shoulders.

I leaned over to place my hand upon those cold, tight fists. "He can look like whatever you wish him to, Sarah. He's not here to win a beauty contest. He's here to help you heal."

"No, it's not that. I've seen him," she whispered. "He's scared the hell out of me! He looks more like a phantom than an angel."

And, for those who haven't formally met Cassiel, he can cause quite a startle. Of all the archangels I've met so far, he's the only one who has appeared to me in the physical world, usually appearing in the moonlit corners of dark rooms or sitting in a barren, moonlit tree during the autumn with his owl or raven. He can even appear solid, with a ghostly complexion and piercing silver eyes. But let me assure you, he is one of the gentlest of souls, urging us to come to terms with our fears, especially our fears of victimization.

Cassiel offers his strength to those who feel weak and his comfort to those who feel alone or antagonized. I have found him to be the patron angel of those who suffer at the hands of abusers, offering his love, compassion, and protection to those in need. He is soft spoken and an angel of few words, but his shoulders are strong, his wings are warm, and he will not let the deeds of those who abuse others erode our spirit.

During the last half of the consultation, Sarah admitted that she actually remembered the last time she cried. It was after a falling out with a high school friend. She said there was so much salt in her tears that they burned welts into her cheeks that didn't heal for days. The visible scarring only made her the target of her family's wrath once again, and from that moment on, she vowed to never shed another tear.

"Never" must have arrived that Sunday. She bowed her head, her shoulders trembling as sobs came forth. She was a highly successful business owner, but admitted that she had to be so that she could be her own boss. She had deep issues about dealing with authority figures, either men or women, and ran her business with an iron fist, leaving little room for error on the part of her employees. Because of her inability to trust that others could do the jobs she delegated, she hadn't taken a vacation in nearly a decade and the stress brought on by her workaholic nature was starting to adversely affect her health.

She told me all of this through tears, and I watched through my own tears as Cassiel wrapped his dark wings around her. I was dismissed by the angel, and I quietly left Sarah in the candlelit room to begin a healing process that would take perhaps years. But I walked away knowing that Cassiel would stay by her side, urging her to let go of her fears so that she might live free of the cruelty her family had beset upon her so long ago.

So, as heavy as he seems, why is Cassiel my favorite angel? I think Sarah's reaction to his appearance hammered it home for me. He's the black sheep of the angel realm, choosing to dwell in the nighttime and work by shadow and moonlight. White robes are certainly not his wardrobe of choice; instead, he prefers a black leather trench coat, tattered black denim jeans, and combat boots. In other words, he just doesn't fit the description of archangel—at least not on first appearance—and surely he must know this. But does that knowing force him to change, to fit into what we as humans believe angels should look like? No. Why should he change? He's just as capable as Michael, Raphael, and Gabriel of carrying out his angelic duties, and to his credit, he looks cooler doing it.

Cassiel comes across as a beautiful, childlike soul who wants to rid us of fear. He uses his sometimes frightening appearance to say, "Judge me by my heart, not my appearance." He's a Renaissance angel if there ever was one, urging us to be open, fair, and accepting of all of God's creatures.

> *If I make a fool of myself, who cares?*
> *I'm not frightened by anyone's perception of me.*
> —ANGELINA JOLIE

ARCHANGEL

METATRON

A WORKER

Whatever you say about Metatron—
the tallest angel in Heaven—
it had better be nice.

—ARCHANGEL MICHAEL

———+———

MEANING OF NAME: Little *YHWH* (a variant of *Yahweh*).

TRIVIA: Metatron is said to be Enoch, a direct descendent of Adam, who did not die but was taken up into Heaven to become an angel. Metatron is the twin brother of Sandalphon.

MESSAGE TO THE CONTEMPORARY WORLD: Behold the Spirit of God that is beautiful and benevolent and dwells within the heart of every child.

PATRON ANGEL (TRADITIONALLY) OF: Children, teachers, librarians, archivists, scribes, storytellers.

PATRON ANGEL (CURRENTLY) OF: The above, plus nannies, babysitters, child psychologists, pediatricians, accountants, bankers.

RULER OF: Monday (Moon); co-rules with Gabriel.

HEAVENLY ASSIGNMENT: Delegated the task of keeping heavenly records, Metatron is associated with the Book of Life and the akashic records.

DEMEANOR WHEN ON THE JOB: Metatron loves children and enjoys teaching.

DEMEANOR WHEN AT PLAY: Metatron is a very playful angel, and enjoys playing with children as well as exchanging lively conversation with adults. Wise and witty, he would be the life of any family reunion.

HUMAN ACCOMPLISHMENTS MOST PROUD OF: All laws governing the protection and welfare of children around the world.

BACK IN THE DAY, HE LIKED: When talent as well as intelligence were rewarded and held in the highest esteem.

TODAY, HE ENJOYS: When children discover and foster their own abilities.

PET PEEVES: Unjust and covetous kings (world leaders); the growing selfishness of modern parents and the related disregard for children as creatures of Spirit, who need dedicated guidance and nurturing.

HOPE FOR THE WORLD (SERIOUS): For it to realize that children are not bargaining chips, nor are they canvases upon which parents can project personal unfulfilled dreams.

HOPE FOR THE WORLD (WHIMSICAL): For people to trade in their video games for sidewalk chalk and learn how to play and socialize with one another. Children would benefit from doing this, too.

IF HE HAD AN ASTROLOGICAL SIGN, IT WOULD BE: Libra.

ELEMENTS: Institutions of education and banking, libraries, books, grassy fields.

GEMSTONES WITH SIMILAR VIBRATION: Agate, crystal quartz, dioptase, malachite-azurite, moonstone, topaz.

FAVORITE SEASON(S): Summer and fall.

ANIMAL TOTEM(S): Puppies, kittens, mice, goldfish.

WING COLOR: Multicolored, rainbow wings; rarely displays them.

FAVORITE ATTIRE: Robes of bright white light (fire); or a white, misty fog.

FAVORITE COLOR(S): All colors.

FAVORITE FOOD(S): Vegetables, as it sets a good example for the children.

FAVORITE MUSIC: A lively fiddle and flute.

IDEAL DATE: A family (or family reunion) baseball game, followed by a picnic, more games, and fireworks.

ASCENDED MASTERS AND BENEVOLENT SPIRIT TEACHERS WITH SIMILAR ENERGY SIGNATURES: Devi, Ganesh, Hotai, St. Nicholas.

NOTABLE PEOPLE WITH SIMILAR VIBRATION: Beverly Cleary, Bill Cosby, Charles Dickens, Walt Disney, Marian Wright Edelman, Jim Henson, Chuck Jones, Nthabeleng Lephoto, Mr. Rogers, Dr. Seuss.

FAVORITE CONTEMPORARY FICTIONAL CHARACTERS: Santa Claus, Mother Goose, Mary Poppins, Pinocchio.

USUALLY ARRIVES IN YOUR LIFE: When you are embarking upon new, uncharted territory in your spiritual journey and are in need of company and security.

METATRON'S MANSION

So where in the world is Metatron? I always think of the theme song to the children's show *Carmen Sandiego* when I think about where exactly Metatron lives. Truth is, he's everywhere, basically. Metatron doesn't have a mansion. Heaven *is* his mansion. After all, the angel is more than a few light-years tall. His bed alone would span the galaxy!

While he might not be tangible, his love is. You can feel his heart and his spirit most in the libraries of the angel metropolis, or further up along the akashic records. I once thought, like many others, that the akashic records were a nineteenth-century myth, a story (which somehow got attached to ancient Egypt and to many other cultures wrapped in mysticism) about a measureless library where every event that happens in the universe is recorded.

Boy, was I wrong. The akashic records are hardly a myth, even though it is said that few people in the world have access to these records (psychic Edgar Cayce being one of them, but that's between Mr. Cayce and Metatron). I do know that the first time I saw the records, Archangel Gabriel pulled me away like a secret service agent pulling a gawker away from an alien crash site.

"You're not ready for that yet," he said in a stern tone. It would be about three years before I finally got a chance to look at the records. When I did, I felt like the dumbest, most illiterate human in existence.

I couldn't understand a damn thing I was reading!

In essence, the akashic records are a monstrous maze of walls—towering walls—of information, upon which is written some sort of digital encrypted data. The information goes by in endless streams like a Wall Street ticker at warp speed, and the characters disappear and reappear. None of it looked familiar to me.

"What the hell am I looking at?" I whined, and I got so dizzy trying to read the script that I could barely keep the meditation going. I had to come out of my lotus pose and lie down. It was then that I heard Metatron chuckle at me with a bit of amusement.

"Need a translator?"

"What's the use of having access to the records if I can't read them?" I groaned and held my head as I spoke to the ceiling.

"You're trying to look at the records with human eyes. You read with your soul, not your eyes, Chantel," Metatron said softly.

"I'd rather have a decoder ring. It'd be a lot easier."

"Get some rest. Try it again tomorrow."

"Nah, that's all right. If I need information that badly, I'll come to you."

"Fair enough. I'm always here should you need me." He chortled. I felt my headache and dizziness fade away and soon after that I fell asleep, only to dream about the digital insanity that was supposed to be the most sophisticated, all-encompassing library in our existence. It is said that those with the gift of claircognizance have open access to the akashic records. The one thing that I've never thought myself very good at is claircognizance, so perhaps it's only fitting that I didn't understand the cyber glyphs whizzing by me like race cars at the Indy 500.

But for those of you with the gift of claircognizance, God bless you, literally. The akashic records are said to be the universe's mainframe computer—the mind of God, if you will—and to access this cybrary is to access everything that can ever been known. Don't forget to take your library card, however, because Metatron, along with his assistant Ramiel, oversees and maintains Heaven's libraries. I don't care how close you say you are to Gabriel or how well you say you know Michael, you ain't getting in without a clearance.

How do you obtain clearance to the Heavenly libraries? It's like this: Don't call Metatron. He'll call you.

> *Never argue with an angel who*
> *is light years taller than you are.*
> —ARCHANGEL RAMIEL

METATRON MANIFEST

I first met Metatron while recuperating from a serious illness. I wasn't working at the time, and was spending a few of my afternoons up at a local teashop where I was afforded the freedom of being myself—a quirky geek who just happened to talk to angels. One day during afternoon tea and a conversation with some locals about angels, I mentioned to the ladies just how militant Gabriel seemed to be, much more so than how he has been depicted throughout history. At the time of my illness, Gabriel was my mentoring angel, and he hadn't taken very much pity on me during the crisis. When I wanted to just fall on my knees and give up, he lifted me. When I cursed Heaven for all the tragedies that had been set upon me, he chastised me. When I had questions about God and my purpose in this world, he answered, but more often than not gave me answers I didn't want to hear. So I spent much of my time with Gabe royally annoyed with him, so much so that I got angry just talking about him.

"You know what? I'm going to talk to his boss," I mused that afternoon. "I want to talk to the higher-ups!" I banged the table, making the teacups rattle. The ladies all laughed at me, but I was serious. Then, as the conversation switched gears and afternoon tea progressed, I felt an immediate shift in the air, like storm clouds were slowly moving in. *Oh darn.*

"Chantel, what is it?" One of the ladies gently took my hand as she saw the discomfort in my eyes. I shook off the feeling and quietly sipped my tea, intermittently gazing up and about the room. I felt like I had just woken a sleeping giant.

Later, when I got home, the giant was waiting for me. The chill that went through my body was enough to make my breath frost up. I hesitantly entered my house, wondering what or who awaited me.

Come on in, there's nothing to fear, little one. The deep voice resounded in my head.

"Little? I'm hardly little." I sat and closed my eyes to better see who I was talking to. All I could see was a dense, white mist. I craned my head upward, gazing into the fog, unable to see much of anything. But slowly something came into focus from above. As it lowered, it looked like a great, billowing cloud, but once it landed in front of me, I realized it was a hand—with fingers twice as big as I am (and I'm a big gal). Its palm was big enough for me to sit in the middle of; I felt like a baby lima bean.

"You're here because of my comment about Gabriel, aren't you? I take it back." I couldn't stop shaking! If ever there was a time I regretted what I'd asked for, this was it. But despite my genuine fear, the angel laughed heartily and then gently invited me to climb upon his hand. I tell you, it's a fat girl's dream to get picked up by a man like she weighs no more than an empty Starbucks coffee cup.

I searched my memory for who this angel could possibly be. Finally, as if whispered, it came to me: *Metatron.*

"Metatron, listen. I'm sorry about what I said back there at the shop. I really didn't mean it."

"Yes, you did." He cradled me in his hand and all my fears were instantly gone. I felt like a little girl sitting on Santa's knee, giddy and confident I could convince St. Nick that I had indeed been a good girl all year.

"Well, maybe if Gabriel weren't so ... "

"Disciplined? Chantel, right now you need that more than ever. Do not begrudge your time with him. He is a very good teacher and you will thank him one day for this."

"I doubt it," I mumbled and curled up in his palm. Metatron and I talked for hours that night, and though I never saw his face, I could hear a smile in his voice. For the first time since my father passed away years ago, I felt that strong sense of protection that all little girls yearn for. In fact, I felt so comforted that I fell into a peaceful sleep, something I hadn't done in the months since my health crisis began.

Metatron is said to be one of the tallest angels in heaven. I certainly can attest to the truth of that claim. But another interesting note about Metatron is that he and his twin brother, Sandalphon, are the babies of the angelic family (since they both manifested after Creation had come into existence). As Heaven's latecomers, neither Metatron nor Sandalphon's names end in the usual suffix of –el, which means "of God" (Gabri-el, Micha-el, Rapha-el). Still, because of Metatron's virtuous deeds on Earth as the biblical Enoch, he was rewarded with a name that many scholars believe means Little *YHWH*, a lesser version of *Yahweh*, the God of Israel. If the tallest angel in Heaven, only measurable by light years according to Archangel Ramiel, is called "little," I doubt one can even fathom how tall God is.

An advocate of children and education, Metatron comes across as a loving father figure who accompanies us on journeys of exploration, whether physically, mentally or spiritually. As a guide, he not only provides direction and insight, but offers his jovial company, since most journeys of self-discovery tend to be lonely ones. Whenever you find yourself at life's crossroads, fearful of the choices you may have to make, know that Metatron is watching over you and will help you to understand and learn from whatever choices you do make, regardless of the consequences. He is not an angel of judgment, but an angel of experience. He graciously extends to all of us feelings of security and surefootedness when we actively seek to understand the life script that we have written out for ourselves.

And who better to accompany us on our journeys than the angel who oversees the Book of Life as well as the akashic records? I've learned quite a few things from Metatron since he first appeared to me. Well, since his hand first appeared to me—that's all I've ever seen of him. Metatron is an angel of temperance, diligence, and patience, and demands these qualities in those he connects with. During the course of this book, Metatron gently nudged me when I was feeling a bit lazy about the project or when I was frustrated with some of the research and things weren't coming together the way I wanted them to. He also taught me about the delicate balance between work, play, and rest.

"No one sleeps anymore," he said to me one evening while I was on the way home from visiting a friend. It was about nine p.m. and the grocery stores were open, their parking lot lights illuminating the night sky. A gas station sign proudly flashed that the station was open twenty-four hours. Starbucks would be open until midnight and Taco Bell had no intention of closing until the wee hours of the morning. All the while, Metatron observed how there was too much work and play and not enough rest in our society. While he philosophized, I quietly pondered playing a few games of solitaire on the computer before even thinking about going to bed that night.

"It's like everyone says, Metatron: I'll sleep when I'm dead," I groaned.

"That's just the thing; sleep doesn't exist beyond the human realm."

"So all those hours I spent trying to beat the timer in Solitaire ... ?"

"Gone, little one. There's no making up for it."

"Damn." I exhaled. But did that stop me from spending about three hours online gaming that night? Not a chance. I didn't learn the true essence of rest until I began heavy research for several projects and learned the hard way that if the body is not well rested, it's not much use. And no, coffee doesn't help the situation. When we're tired, we should sleep! How difficult is that to understand?

Well, apparently it's a novel idea since not enough people make time for it. But know that if Metatron shows up by your side, one of two things is going to happen: you'll either heed his instruction and listen to your body when it needs rest, or you'll heed his instruction the hard way—which can come in the form of the flu, a broken leg, a layoff, or anything else you may have hidden away in your life script. It's all about building our physical, emotional, and mental stamina for our continued journey through this existence, so that we get the best possible benefit from every situation and experience we encounter.

> *Sleep is the best meditation.*
> —DALAI LAMA

ARCHANGEL

RAMIEL

A WORKER

With Ramiel around, nothing is off the record.

—ARCHANGEL GABRIEL

———+———

MEANING OF NAME: God's mercy.

TRIVIA: On Judgment Day, Ramiel shepherds souls before the
Heavenly Throne. He and Uriel look forward to being tag-
team wranglers on the Day of Reckoning.

MESSAGE TO THE CONTEMPORARY WORLD: The only history a human can ever be certain of is that which he makes himself.

PATRON ANGEL (TRADITIONALLY) OF: Tribal elders, shamans,
prophets, family elders, archivists, librarians, historians,
educators.

PATRON ANGEL (CURRENTLY) OF: The above, plus history museum curators, archeologists, forensic specialists, statisti-
cians, stenographers, and stock market and economic ana-
lysts.

RULER OF: Thursday (Jupiter); co-rules with Chamuel.

HEAVENLY ASSIGNMENT: Ramiel maintains the chronicles of both Heaven and Earth.

DEMEANOR WHEN ON THE JOB: Reserved, Ramiel observes all that transpires with an objective view.

DEMEANOR WHEN AT PLAY: Ramiel's work is never done, but his favorite pastime is predicting human events based purely on historical patterns.

HUMAN ACCOMPLISHMENTS MOST PROUD OF: The sundial, typewriter, atomic clock, Big Ben, portable video camera.

BACK IN THE DAY, HE LIKED: The art of maintaining tribal history by orally passing it from one generation to the next.

TODAY, HE ENJOYS: Watching the art of journaling return. "Electronic mail has eroded the art of letter writing, but blogging has taken diary writing to a whole new level; and it is a good thing when humans exchange ideas, concepts, and opinions."

PET PEEVE: The altering or distortion of historical facts, as it is usually for material or political gain.

HOPE FOR THE WORLD (SERIOUS): For it to understand that history is not a composite of stories written in tomes, but a navigational map to help succeeding generations avoid life's snares and pitfalls.

HOPE FOR THE WORLD (WHIMSICAL): For it to make judgments based on facts and rationality instead of opinions and the egocentric need to be right.

IF HE HAD AN ASTROLOGICAL SIGN, IT WOULD BE: Aquarius.

ELEMENTS: Trees, rocks, soil, paper (parchment, papyrus, and rice), writing instruments, clocks, calendars, any instrument that aids in historical research and documenting.

GEMSTONES WITH SIMILAR VIBRATION: Agate, alexandrite, cat's eye, crystal quartz, sodalite.

FAVORITE SEASON(S): All seasons.

ANIMAL TOTEM(S): Owl.

WING COLOR: Doesn't display them.

FAVORITE ATTIRE: Wool robes of earth tones.

FAVORITE COLORS: Earth colors.

FAVORITE FOOD: Manna (food of angels).

FAVORITE MUSIC: Renaissance.

IDEAL DATE: A sunrise hymn at Stonehenge during the summer solstice, followed by breakfast in Egypt with a view of the pyramids.

ASCENDED MASTERS AND BENEVOLENT SPIRIT TEACHERS WITH SIMILAR ENERGY SIGNATURES: Chronos, Janus, Father Time/Baby New Year, Noah.

NOTABLE PEOPLE WITH SIMILAR VIBRATION: Adam, Benjamin Franklin, Hellen Keller, Toni Morrison, George Noory, George Orwell, J. R. R. Tolkien.

FAVORITE CONTEMPORARY FICTIONAL CHARACTERS: Mr. Spock, R2D2, the Mad Hatter.

USUALLY ARRIVES IN YOUR LIFE: When it's time to revisit your past and recognize your life's patterns in order to facilitate future healing and growth.

RAMIEL'S MANSION

Dark wooden shelves lined with books, illuminated by far too few candles, give Ramiel's mansion a dark and mysterious atmosphere. Breaking up the monotony of the endless span of bookshelves is artwork from across the ages and around the world, along with hanging silver mobiles of hundreds of galaxies I don't recognize. Ramiel's mansion is a scholar's wildest dream, with not only more books than any human could possibly read in a lifetime, but with doorways that lead to each library in Heaven. How many doorways? I lost count around a hundred and ten.

One thing I noticed, outside of the fact it is much too dark to read anything, is that the air is completely still. It is as if the room is holding its breath; I found myself holding my breath on several occasions. There are no windows, no ocean breezes as I had felt in other angelic mansions ... just books and artifacts, an occasional candle, and plenty of sitting room for one angel who never seems to be home. Since Ramiel works in a library, you would think that the last thing he'd want to see is more books when he gets home. But then again, the one thing we humans can count on is angels being consistent. They are who they are, no matter where they are.

RAMIEL MANIFEST

Archangel Ramiel shares his scribing duties with Archangel Metatron. While Metatron seems to prefer a more digital way of maintaining records (the akashic cybrary), Ramiel prefers the old-fashioned quill and inkwell. On the day of his interview, he gave me a glimpse of one of the countless libraries he maintains. I expected great pillars of alabaster and books shelved away on white, billowing clouds—you know, a Heavenly library. But what I saw instead was a structure the size of a large metropolis, locked in silence. There were no walls, just shelves, some of them spanning up and into the sunlit clouds above. Equally as astonishing were the books themselves, bound in leathery material and as big as compact cars turned upright on their bumpers. I would need an industrial-sized crane just to extract one from the shelves, so my hopes of casually flipping through one were quickly dashed. I seriously doubt, however, that the angels in all their strength and ingenuity would have a difficult time of it.

"So, how many trees were slaughtered for this one right here?" I pointed to a book that was about six feet thick.

"You're funny," Ramiel quipped, leading me through the endless maze until we arrived at a sitting area with large reading tables surrounded by a vibrant garden of roses. Why there were tables there, I didn't bother to ask. It wasn't like any of the books could fit on any of them. As with some of the other things I've come to notice about the angels, I attributed it all to the creation of appearances.

"So what language are these books written in?"

"Every written language there is," Ramiel boasted.

"Oh, so *you're* the ones who inspired those crazy instruction manuals written in ten different languages! Do you know how difficult it is to flip through one of those?"

"Well, fortunately for us, we don't have to turn the book upside down and flip the book backwards, as it were," he chuckled. As I looked in awe of the impressive arrangement, I realized that beyond a few helper angels, Ramiel and Metatron run the whole show as far as documenting everything in the cosmos (from your tirade at McDonald's because they put pickles on your hamburger to little Suzie's tirade at Toys "R" Us clear across town because they were out of miniature tea sets).

My hands tucked deep in my pockets, I walked down an aisle; none of the books I saw had English titles. I figured that the English language section was a few miles down, across a bridge, past the park, and immediately to the left of the second light. Or something like that.

"Talk about downsizing. Only two archangels are delegated to do all this work? I'd talk to labor relations if I were you."

"We manage just fine." Ramiel casually followed me and I was grateful, just in case I got lost.

"You know, Ramiel, that's taking jobs away from resident angels who direly need to work." I grinned impishly over my shoulder at him.

"Behave," he growled back, and I shrugged innocently as I continued my tour. It's true that Ramiel's work is never done, but one interest he shared with me along the tour was that he enjoys calculating human events based on historical patterns. *What, angels don't know the future?*

Compared to humans, angels can see light years ahead, but they don't know everything where the Creator's plans are concerned. The angels are only given the information they need at the time they need it. Don't worry, they can see well into your future and beyond, but when Ramiel comes to the foreground of your life, he is there to help you review your past experiences so the insight can be used for experiences yet to come.

Ever find yourself in a tense situation only to pause, look at your surroundings, and say, "I went through this mess five years ago!" That mess could have been an unhealthy relationship, family upheaval, or stressful work conditions. Regardless of what the situation was, you recognized that you had gone through it once, twice, and (for some of us hard-of-learning), three or four times. This is the work of Ramiel, beckoning you to look at what you did not learn the first time around so that you *get it* the next time. He helps us to recognize life patterns and our emotional habits so, at the very least, we will know what not to do in the future.

Ramiel is not an angel of action who interacts with us heavily. He merely whispers clues to us along the way, provoking us to ponder where we've come from, where we are, and where we're headed. He encourages us above all to be honest with ourselves, to stand back and take an objective view of our lives. It's this type of personal assessment, every other season or so, that ultimately reveals to us our life's purpose, and gives us glimpses into our life scripts.

> *Time will explain it all. He is a talker,*
> *and needs no questioning before he speaks.*
> —EURIPIDES

HEAVENLY ASSIGNMENT: Raguel is like a department manager, who receives work orders from the Heavenly Throne and then distributes them among the archangels.

DEMEANOR WHEN ON THE JOB: High-octane, laser-focused. Michael says Raguel works so fast that not even the angels can see him most times.

DEMEANOR WHEN AT PLAY: Doesn't play. "I'm married to my job and we have a meaningful and fulfilling relationship."

HUMAN ACCOMPLISHMENTS MOST PROUD OF: Industrial developments that are socially and environmentally conscious.

BACK IN THE DAY, HE LIKED: Honest, noble men who worked hard to earn their keep.

TODAY, HE ENJOYS: The same, but they're few and far between these days.

PET PEEVE: Slave labor. "You would think that after what happened with the *Egypt vs. Moses* incident, humanity would have gotten a clue, but *nooooo*."

HOPE FOR THE WORLD (SERIOUS): For it to implement and enforce the philosophy that every man and woman deserves the opportunity to work and earn decent wages to feed and adequately support a family.

HOPE FOR THE WORLD (WHIMSICAL): Every business should have an annual picnic where the head supervisors are targets in either a pie-throwing competition or a dunk tank. It improves employee morale and keeps leaders humble.

IF HE HAD AN ASTROLOGICAL SIGN, IT WOULD BE: Pisces.

ELEMENTS: Steam, heat, energy, industry, community, fruit trees, agriculture.

GEMSTONES WITH SIMILAR VIBRATION: Agate, amazonite, chrysocolla, crystal quartz, gold calcite, onyx, smoky quartz, tiger's eye.

FAVORITE SEASON(S): Fall.

ANIMAL TOTEM(S): Beasts of burden.

WING COLOR: Royal blue.

FAVORITE ATTIRE: Deep blue angel robes and an endless stack of parchment work orders.

FAVORITE COLOR(S): Blue. "It's a very industrious color."

FAVORITE FOOD(S): "Coffee. Just kidding." Has a "strange" affinity for olives … all kinds! Enjoys the flavors of the Mediterranean and the Middle East.

FAVORITE MUSIC: Sounds of nature.

IDEAL DATE: Not interested.

ASCENDED MASTERS AND BENEVOLENT SPIRIT TEACHERS WITH SIMILAR ENERGY SIGNATURES: Lu-Hsing, Moses, Solomon.

NOTABLE PEOPLE WITH SIMILAR VIBRATION: Margaret "Unsinkable Molly" Brown, Thomas Edison, Henry Ford, Morgan

Freeman, Bill Gates, Martin Luther King Jr., Abraham Lincoln, Eleanor Roosevelt, Martha Stewart, Rex David "Dave" Thomas, Ted Turner, Orson Welles.

FAVORITE CONTEMPORARY FICTIONAL CHARACTERS: Ebenezer Scrooge—"He had to be a miser in the beginning to get a scope of just how big his heart truly was in the end."

USUALLY ARRIVES IN YOUR LIFE: When it's time to reorganize your priorities and get down to business.

RAGUEL'S MANSION

All the angelic mansions have their own unique blend of styles, but Raguel's is the only one that looks like it could be part of an American or Japanese industrial park. A version of a Mesopotamian ziggurat dressed up for the computer age, this mansion is an elaborately layered pyramid of white limestone with windows as blue as the ocean—or as green, depending on the position of the sun.

The land around the structure is a meticulously manicured maze of shrubs and trees, with pristine white pathways that I don't feel comfortable walking on lest my shoes leave a scuff. For a building that looks like it houses hundreds, if not thousands, of cubicle-bound workers, it is as peaceful as Chamuel's Zen garden. When I entered the foyer, I was met by a lavish, indoor waterfall three stories high, embedded in a landscape of tropical plants. Beyond that was a sleek yet simple motif of black and white marble.

Though there wasn't a soul in sight, the ziggurat still felt alive and buzzing with energy, and once I was away from the sounds of the waterfall, I could hear that all the corridors were filled with a faint hum, as if countless computers and machines were working away behind closed doors. Or maybe the sound wasn't mechanical at all, but Raguel's presence. For all I know, since he's one of the fastest angels in Heaven, he could have been there and left several times while I snuck around. Every now and then, out the corner of my eye, I would see a tiny white or gold sphere whizzing about like a comet. It would go down a hall and I'd chase it, but it would quickly hook a corner and disappear. I called out to it several times, but it seemed to ignore me as it went on about its business, whatever that was.

While touring this office building that seemed far too beautiful to be empty, I had to constantly remind myself that I was in an angelic mansion and not the headquarters of some mega-monolithic corporation. So I simply strolled along, noting how the mansion reflected Raguel's style: exacting, organized, efficient, and reticent. Not a single door was unlocked! I walked up and down long corridors, each one as monotone as the next with its closed doors, shiny doorknobs, and the incessant humming. It was worse than walking through the Pentagon during Christmas break would be, and it reminded me of something I'd felt about Raguel on occasion: the angel could talk for hours and never tell you anything about what's going on in Heaven, not a hint or a clue.

And so it was with his mansion; it was not about to offer up a single secret—for the sake of Heavenly security, I'm sure. Of course, I could get into the building and take in the tranquility of the tropical waterfall. I could ride the elevators up and down all day—elevators that had no buttons, by the way, and just randomly put me on a floor to explore more closed doors. I could walk that mansion from sun-up to sundown and not see a single thing, not even a coffeemaker. What office complex doesn't have a coffee maker, or even the scent of microwaved popcorn wafting into the halls?

I'm sure Raguel likes his mansion as still and silent as a stone and as secure as the U.S. Federal Reserve. I didn't take it personally that I couldn't see much or that I didn't get a VIP tour. I've a feeling that anyone who shows up without an appointment won't get far, whether human or angel.

Next time, I'll make an appointment and I'll take my own coffee.

RAGUEL MANIFEST

When I said early in this book that you can talk to your angels anytime and anywhere, I meant it. The following interview with Raguel took place on a stormy Tuesday afternoon at one of my favorite Chinese restaurants. Now, while it's perfectly acceptable to talk to your angels, be careful while doing it in public. My only saving grace that afternoon was that my hair was hanging loose over my ears, so if a chuckle escaped during the otherwise silent interview (done through clairaudience), I just tilted my head and pressed my fingers to my ear as if I were listening to a wireless cell phone earpiece.

Raguel was one of the last two angels I hunted down to interview. I spent days summoning him, sending reminders that I had a deadline for this project and that he, along with Sandalphon, were holding up the train. Granted, I had been lazily and infrequently working on the book, but one would think that since I was now ready to complete the project, the angels would come running to my immediate aid. Raguel proved me wrong.

I was very close to cutting this archangel from my final list of angels when I decided to take an afternoon, sit at my favorite restaurant, and edit the book. It was then that Raguel suddenly appeared out of nowhere to add his input. I was relieved at his arrival, but still miffed that he had seemed to ignore me for weeks! I really wanted to say, "What the heck took you so long?" But I realized that Raguel is one of the busiest archangels in Heaven, so I let it slide.

I could tell right from the start that Raguel was not one for casual chitchat, so I thought that turning our meeting into a formal interview would be best for both of us. He is the patron angel of "taking care of business," so I felt that a structured yet concise Q&A would suit him best.

C. In a nutshell, you're the archangel of business, labor, and industry. With that, I know you're on the clock, so I won't take up much of your time.

R. Time? Ha! You've been hanging around Ramiel too long. You humans are bound by time. We angels are not.

C. I find it interesting that your area of governance is business, but when I wrote down "Stock Exchange" in my notes, you put the brakes on. Why?

R. Stock exchanges are games. They're more like gambling than actual business. Talk to Sandalphon, he likes that sort of stuff.

C. I did, but he doesn't want to touch that realm.

R. Eh, he's not big on competition. Michael maybe?

C. Dunno, I'll ask. Speaking of Michael, he told me that you move so fast that not even the angels can see you. How many work orders can there possibly be in a day? Don't you get a break or go on a vacation?

R. Firstly, Chantel, you're thinking in terms of linear time. The universe doesn't function in that manner. Everything works in an instant, simultaneously! There is no past or present or future. There is only now, and right now, I've distributed more work orders than any human could ever count.

C. Right now? As in *right now* right now? You mean while we're sitting here, talking?

R. Exactly.

C. Okay. Even so, Speedy, how many work orders are there? There are only six billion people on this planet.

R. "Only." I like that you realize that six billion is a relatively tiny number. But the archangels don't interact just with humans—there's nature and other elements to tend to.

C. Still, Raguel, you're archangels. How hard can it be to watch over this planet?

R. Just when I was about to give you an "A" for observation (he leaned in closer). You're under the assumption that this planet, this reality, is the only reality.

C. Raguel, suffice it to say that it's the only one I've seen.

R. Not true! Completely untrue! You wrote about the mansions. Gabriel's taken you on tours. I know; I processed those requests.

C. (Laughs) Yeah, but . . .

R. But nothing, Chantel. There are more worlds than any human could imagine, and we angels work to keep these worlds running efficiently. Iophiel would say "in perfect harmony," but whatever.

C. I don't know. Some people would say that you guys are going a shoddy job of keeping this world in harmony. I can't speak for other worlds, as you put it, but this one seems seriously out of whack.

R. See, that's an observation best proposed to Uriel or Gabriel. I just work here (chuckle). Besides, there is no one in your world who was forced to exist there. There are plenty of less turbulent realms, just as there are more turbulent realms, and you could have chosen to go to any of them. But no, you came here, so don't complain.

C. I'm not complaining! Well, at least not much.

R. Listen, next time choose a tropical planet and create a reality where you get beachfront property.

C. I can do that? Seriously, Raguel.

R. Everyone can do that! I process every life request for approval. Some of them I read and say, "Why? Why are you choosing *that* realm?"

C. Well, six billion of us can't be wrong, Raguel.

R. No, it's just that six billion of you like drama way too much. It could be worse, though; there are other places much more perilous.

C. Would Hell be one of those places?

R. Hell is a point of view, Chantel. But if you're thinking of Hell in terms of a place of strife, pestilence, and torment, then yes, there are worlds I would dub "Hell."

C. Well, why do those worlds even exist? Why would anyone want to go there?

R. The worlds exist for the sake of experience, for the sake of learning. I mean, why would a human want to jump out of an airplane, climb a mountain, fly a kite during a thunderstorm?

C. Okay, the whole kite-flying thing was experimentation that led to some great discoveries.

R. Yes, go on.

C. The other two, well, that's for the sake of thrill. Tests of stamina, maybe?

R. There you go. The worlds exist for all those things.

C. Wow, that's um … wow, Raguel. All this just because we want to?

R. That and because you can. Make no mistake, though. Whether you're here in a quest for discovery or simply for the thrill of it, it does not in any way demean your life's purpose. It's the journey itself that is the meaning of life. You are all affecting each other, creating causes, and engaging in experiences with one another. You still walk away with lessons learned, memories, feelings.

Nothing is trivial. If it's any consolation, everyone gets out alive and unscathed.

C. Uh, tell that to the gravediggers of the world, Raguel. A lot of people would disagree and I'm one of them.

R. Chantel, this isn't life. It's a single experience within the span of eternity. That's all. Once you're done with this experience, you'll move right into another ... of your choosing, of course.

C. I have to say that I'm a bit wary of that notion still. I mean, knowing all of this doesn't make me feel any better about dying.

R. It's not going to, unless that's the way you set up your life script. Those who are supposed to understand this will, and those who aren't, won't. It's just that simple.

C. Well, I'm not coming this way again. I'll sign up for the beachfront on that tropical planet you mentioned.

R. Sure. You always say that, Chantel. You know, we've really moved into Uriel's realm here.

C. I know, but I appreciate you sharing your insight all the same. Any final thoughts?

R. Yes. You're lucky it was Raphael and not I who came to you about this book. If it had been me, you would have gotten it done in five months instead of five years.

C. Ah ha! But if I knew ahead of time that I was going to be a procrastinator in this lifetime, then it was only right

that I ask gentle and patient Raphael to come to me
instead of Heaven's resident workaholic.

R. Touché.

Raguel and I then went on to discuss how humans pursue the
meaning of life as if they will discover something truly unique
and profound; people are hyper-focused on the destination
instead of the journey. But the crux of it all is the journey. It's
why we're all here—to engage the senses and the emotions
and experience an existence where we aren't in a state of full
knowing, where we are at the mercy of the elements around
us. It's the ultimate survival challenge to see what we're made
of. As spiritual beings, we're aware of our increased strength
and knowledge, but how do we fair when we're plunked in the
middle of the arena without all our divine capabilities?

To say the least, it certainly makes things interesting. Some
of us will return to our spirit lives with new emotions, or new
insights into our spiritual selves. Others will shake off this existence like a rider getting off a roller-coaster, with arms in the
air and a scream of victory: "I made it out in one piece!" Smil-
ing, with the adrenaline pumping, they'll bravely run to the
next ride, eager to test the limitations of being human. Raguel
will be standing dutifully at the ride's entrance, with a height
chart to see if they meet the requirements.

But that's on the spiritual side. Here on the human side,
Raguel comes into our lives when it's time to start taking our

personal goals more seriously. Nothing agitates this archangel more than apathy, complacency, and loafing around, and he has no problem letting you know when you've dawdled long enough and it's time to buckle down and accomplish more from a "To Do" list than the act of writing it. Whether the goal is to lose weight, put away extra funds for rainy days, meditate regularly, or clean out the garage, Raguel comes to the fore to push us into productivity and therefore to progress. He is a procrastinator's worst nightmare—as he will not only speed up time, but place obstacles in your way to teach you the lesson of "next time, start on time." (Hence, his absence during the crunch time when I felt I needed him most.)

I know to be a bit more concerted, next time, in my efforts when working toward a goal. I've a sinking feeling that I've not heard the last of Raguel. Since the interview, I've promised myself to be more mindful and avoid procrastination in the future.

If such a future even exits.

> *I've never run into a guy who could win at the top level*
> *in anything today and didn't have the right attitude,*
> *didn't give it everything he had at least while he was*
> *doing it, wasn't prepared and didn't have the whole*
> *program worked out.*
>
> —TED TURNER

ARCHANGEL

GABRIEL

AN INTERCESSOR

Gabriel's trumpet is more menacing than Michael's war cry.

—Archangel Cassiel

———————

Meaning of name: God is my strength.

Trivia: In biblical lore, Gabriel announced to the Virgin Mary that she was to be the mother of the Messiah, Jesus Christ.

Message to the contemporary world: True liberation comes not by surrendering to either humans or machines, but to the Divine Order of the universe.

Patron angel (traditionally) of: Writers, orators, philosophers, theologians, actors, poets.

Patron angel (currently) of: The above, plus physicists, computer geeks, bloggers, entrepreneurs, life coaches, motivational speakers.

Ruler of: Monday (Moon); co-rules with Metatron.

HEAVENLY ASSIGNMENT: The go-between for humankind and God.

DEMEANOR WHEN ON THE JOB: Gabriel is more militant and less jovial than Michael, who is the patron of warriors.

DEMEANOR WHEN AT PLAY: Gabriel doesn't play much, but he is often the victim of his brother Michael's harmless pranks.

HUMAN ACCOMPLISHMENTS MOST PROUD OF: Smoke signals, drum signals, the telegraph, the telephone, the Internet.

BACK IN THE DAY, HE ADMIRED: Leonardo da Vinci.

TODAY, HE ADMIRES: Steven Hawking.

PET PEEVE: Humanity's inability to be objective.

HOPE FOR THE WORLD (SERIOUS): For it to embrace philosophy and intellectual discourse once again.

HOPE FOR THE WORLD (WHIMSICAL): For it to turn off the television and pick up a book.

IF HE HAD AN ASTROLOGICAL SIGN, IT WOULD BE: Gemini.

ELEMENTS: Air, mountains, radio waves, fiber optics, wind, string and wind instruments.

GEMSTONES WITH SIMILAR VIBRATION: Agate, azurite, citrine, crystal quartz, rutilated quartz, sapphire.

FAVORITE SEASON(S): Spring and summer.

ANIMAL TOTEM(S): None mentioned.

WING COLOR: Beige/tan with threads of gold.

FAVORITE ATTIRE: Formal white robes, with creases just so.

FAVORITE COLOR(S): Cream, beige, linen, gold.

FAVORITE FOOD(S): Manna (food of angels).

FAVORITE MUSIC: Traditional Indian and European Renaissance.

IDEAL DATE: A day at the art museum, followed by dinner at home.

ASCENDED MASTERS AND BENEVOLENT SPIRIT TEACHERS WITH SIMILAR ENERGY SIGNATURES: Confucius, Jesus, Mother Mary Queen of Angels, St. Germain, Siddhartha Gautama Buddha.

NOTABLE PEOPLE WITH SIMILAR VIBRATION: Maya Angelou, St. Thomas Aquinas, Jane Austen, Kenneth Branagh, Dalai Lama, Albert Einstein, Gandhi, Steven Hawking, Joan of Arc, Mother Teresa, Sappho, Shakespeare, Phyllis Wheatley.

FAVORITE CONTEMPORARY FICTIONAL CHARACTERS: No preference.

USUALLY ARRIVES IN YOUR LIFE: When you begin to question your place in God's Great Equation and want to take a conscious role in fulfilling your life's purpose.

GABRIEL'S MANSION

To enter Gabriel's mansion is to become emerged in the ancient days of Greece—with its towering limestone pillars and vast open spaces.

Linen banners flow gracefully between the columns and Gabriel's favorite pieces of battle armor stand on display, either alone or worn by the statues of his many angelic brothers. These marble and limestone statues tower high overhead, commanding attention and awe, but they're not stationary. I've been to Gabriel's mansion several times, and have discovered that the statues are not permanent fixtures. But the mystery behind the disappearing, reappearing statues remains to be solved.

In marble floors so glossy you can see your own reflection, I was given a glimpse into Gabriel's exacting nature, as well as into his adoration of beauty and form. For an angel whose element is air, it is only fitting that there isn't a single closed space in this angelic Parthenon—there's only a view of a shimmering blue ocean, a gently flowing sea breeze, and a sun high overhead that never sets.

> *Yeah, I tell everyone to chill out and lighten up,*
> *especially Gabriel.*
> —ARCHANGEL MICHAEL

GABRIeL MAnifeST

When Gabriel appears in a reading, I tell my client both "congratulations" and "my condolences" in the same breath. Gabriel is known by many as The Messenger, and is the patron saint of writers, actors, journalists, and anyone else in the communication fields. But he's so much deeper than that. When Gabriel comes into your life, he is there because you are about to embark on a long and challenging spiritual journey. He is there when you arrive at the point in your life where you start asking the big questions: *Who am I? Why am I here? What's my purpose?* When you start asking these questions and seeking serious answers, Gabriel moves into the foreground of your life to help you discover the real you—your spiritual Self, your spiritual identity.

Also, when it comes to dealing with internal changes (changes in thoughts, beliefs, personalities, etc.), Gabriel is there leading the way. You may stumble a few times in this journey of self-exploration, but Gabriel will never let you fall.

I liken Gabriel to the spiritual personal trainer, the motivator, who out of dedication bellows orders and demands improvement at every turn. These periods of self-examination are a lot like weight training. To get into shape, you may start out with a ten- or fifteen-pound weight. But after so many weeks, you eventually have to move to twenty pounds, then thirty, fifty, and so on. Self-awareness (which serves as a bridge, a conscious connection between you and the Creator) does not make your life easier. Quite the contrary; the challenges will begin to mount.

These challenges are what push people back, forcing them to retreat in fear and self-pity. Many people entertain the notion that the closer you are to God, the easier life will be. I have found that the closer you get to God, the more challenges you face, but you will be stronger and have a better stamina to endure them. And this is why Gabriel is so vocal and so willing to show signs to reinforce your faith in yourself. He is the angel of inspiration and motivation, and will help you climb your way toward greater spiritual understanding.

As I mentioned earlier, connecting to the Creator requires surrender, and only your Higher Self and God know just how much of that you can handle. Gabriel is not there just to make sure you don't buckle under the pressure, but to show you blessings you would otherwise overlook because you are so overwhelmed by the changes and challenges taking place in your life.

I have said many times, "When Gabriel says jump, just ask 'how high?'" He is not one to be ignored. Well, none of the angels are, but if you ignore Gabriel's instructions, he will surely allow you to see the error of your ways. He is supportive but demanding, like any sports coach who is determined to see his team win. So when you find yourself, in the middle of your journey, butting heads with Gabriel—because it *will* happen—just remember these pointers:

Never argue with Gabriel. You will lose. He is the archangel of communication and rules the throat and voice.

Talk to him. He will respond. Gabriel's voice is soothing, and you will always hear him in your right ear. Listen to him. He will never tell you to harm anyone or yourself or to do things against the inherent good nature of your soul.

Ask for help, signs, timelines, deadlines—whatever you can. Gabriel may not provide them all, but he will always give you just enough information to work with. And even if you feel it is insufficient, just thank him, surrender, and continue to move forward.

Gabriel never angers, but has no problem telling you when to shut up and stop complaining about things not going your way. Watch this especially while driving, lest a four-legged forest furball runs out in front of your car. Gabriel will get your attention any way he can, even if it means making your heart jump into your throat.

Though Gabriel can be a bit abrasive—and sometimes brutally honest—he is still an angel. Keep in mind that he is here for your growth. By any means necessary, he will keep his vow to help you fulfill your purpose.

Gabriel is a master of patience. You best start learning patience too if you are to avoid many a headache while working with him.

> *If you don't like something, change it.*
> *If you can't change it, change your attitude.*
> *Don't complain.*
> —MAYA ANGELOU

ARCHANGEL

SANDALPHON

AN INTERCESSOR

There is no sweeter melody than the sound of Sandalphon's heart.

—ARCHANGEL IOPHIEL

———

MEANING OF NAME: Brother.

TRIVIA: Sandalphon is said to be the Hebrew prophet Elijah, who did not taste death but was caught up in a chariot of fire and taken up to Heaven to become an angel. Sandalphon's twin brother is Metatron.

MESSAGE TO THE CONTEMPORARY WORLD: If humans didn't shield the radiance of the Spirit in their hearts, there would be no need for sunlight.

PATRON ANGEL (TRADITIONALLY) OF: Prayer, music, law, youth, unborn children.

PATRON ANGEL (CURRENTLY) OF: The above, plus children with disabilities, midwives, concentration, mathematics, playfulness and games (board games, video games), puzzles, riddles, secrets, academics, school exams, gifts and charity, florists.

RULER OF: Friday (Venus); co-rules with Iophiel.

HEAVENLY ASSIGNMENT: To calm, uplift, or enlighten souls through the use of music and the imagination. He is Heaven's Chief Muse.

DEMEANOR WHEN ON THE JOB: Sandalphon has a very playful nature, and will share his uplifting energies with all he encounters.

DEMEANOR WHEN AT PLAY: Focused, but not exceedingly competitive. He'll let you win at a game if you promise to practice more in the future.

HUMAN ACCOMPLISHMENTS MOST PROUD OF: Nothing in particular. Everything has a use.

BACK IN THE DAY, HE LIKED: Stickball and the fact that children spent more time playing together outside than they did doing nothing alone inside.

TODAY, HE ENJOYS: Multiplayer (video/online) games where teamwork and camaraderie is crucial to achieving a goal.

PET PEEVE: Selfish, stingy people, especially when it comes to the welfare of children.

HOPE FOR THE WORLD (SERIOUS): For it to spend more time celebrating life and less time destroying it.

HOPE FOR THE WORLD (WHIMSICAL): For it to solve all major conflicts through chess tournaments. The game of Battleship would be a good runner-up.

IF HE HAD AN ASTROLOGICAL SIGN, IT WOULD BE: Taurus.

ELEMENTS: Grassy fields, wild flowers, playgrounds, all musical instruments, comic books, secret passageways, school buildings, laughter, air, aether.

GEMSTONES WITH SIMILAR VIBRATION: Agate, blue tourmaline, crystal quartz, fluorite.

FAVORITE SEASON(S): All seasons.

ANIMAL TOTEM(S): Nothing in particular.

WING COLOR: Beige and brown. Rarely shows them.

FAVORITE ATTIRE: Simple brown trousers, worn-in shoes, white collar shirt with the sleeves rolled up, and suspenders.

FAVORITE COLOR(S): Sunny, bright colors.

FAVORITE FOOD(S): Anything sweet. Loves candy.

FAVORITE MUSIC: Classical, Jazz, Blues, Soul, Country.

IDEAL DATE: An evening at an amusement park, followed by dinner and fireworks on an old-fashioned riverboat.

ASCENDED MASTERS AND BENEVOLENT SPIRIT TEACHERS WITH SIMILAR ENERGY SIGNATURES: Cherubs, Cupid, Elijah the Prophet, elves and fairies, Hathor, John the Baptist, Kwan Yin, St. Theresa.

NOTABLE PEOPLE WITH SIMILAR VIBRATION: Tim Allen, Louis Armstrong, William "Count" Basie, James Brown, Jim Carey, Charlie Chaplin, Sammy Davis Jr., Judy Garland, Benny Hill, Buster Keaton, Gene Kelly, Michelangelo, Wolfgang Amadeus Mozart, Jack Nicholson, Rachel Ray, Ginger Rogers, Babe Ruth, Shirley Temple, Stevie Ray Vaughan, Weird Al Yankovic.

FAVORITE CONTEMPORARY FICTIONAL CHARACTERS: The Addams Family, Beetlejuice, Forrest Gump, Goonies, Huckleberry Finn, Laurel and Hardy, Little Rascals, Mr. Ed, Peter Pan, Three Stooges.

USUALLY ARRIVES IN YOUR LIFE: When you need to find common ground between work and play. Not all work has to be arduous, and not all play is merely a way to pass the time. To discover the middle ground between the two is to discover a life of perfect harmony.

SANDALPHON'S MANSION

Sandalphon's mansion is probably the homiest of the angelic lot. It certainly looks like human hands had a part in its construction, or maybe, as with all the other mansions, Sandalphon's tastes simply have had noticeable influences in the human world.

Colonial architecture gives his mansion a welcoming atmosphere; when I visited, I felt invited to come in, take a load off, and stay awhile. I didn't doubt that if I had asked for iced tea or lemonade it would have popped up somewhere in the spacious living room, which was decorated in shades of warm brown sugar and cool colonial blue. It was like walking into everything that was Americana—with fluffy patchwork quilts lying about and the scent of apple pie in the air.

Throughout the house, musical instruments sit on display and sheet music lies about. The Philharmonic Orchestra would not be lacking if they ever decide to play at Sandalphon's, since his mansion is also attached to an immense hall that can seat more than an average sports stadium. Just as I was thinking that the acoustics in a place this large would be compromised, logic prompted me to remember where I was—in the home of the Patron of Music. I think Sandalphon has probably accounted for such acoustic technicalities.

I headed away from the orchestra hall and past the main room, clear to the other side of the mansion, where I found the granddaddy of all game rooms—that many a child could get lost in for weeks. From billiards to darts to board games and video games, Sandalphon's play room was what Peter Pan could only fantasize about. There was something for everyone; the room that seemed to span forever, and also had its own ice cream parlor and bottomless bowls of candy. Willy Wonka, eat your heart out.

After a moment of skee-ball, I ventured outdoors and was met with sun-kissed fields of wheat and corn. A baseball field sat just off to the side of the house and in the distance was a crystal blue river with an old-fashioned riverboat sitting at the docks. I didn't know whether to grab a catcher's mitt, a fishing pole, or a deck of poker cards, but what I do know is that when I leave this existence in the human realm, I'll be hanging at Sandalphon's for a while. The angel certainly knows how to have fun, and his mansion seems like a much better place for a birthday party than one of those old pizza parlors with singing robots.

Meet you at the jungle gym.

> *Chess? I'm not impressed by his chess skills.*
> *You wanna impress me, let me see him on the field*
> *for a game of dodgeball.*
> —ARCHANGEL MICHAEL

> *Michael's just sore because he always loses Boardwalk*
> *and Park Place to Sandalphon. My twin brother*
> *isn't called the Master of Games for nothing.*
> —ARCHANGEL METATRON

SANDALPHON MANIFEST

When I began this book, Sandalphon did not make it onto my initial list of twelve angels. I had not yet met him, and he couldn't have been farther from my mind as I focused instead on those angels I interacted with on a regular basis. But as I began my research, I kept running into references to Sandalphon, especially when looking into Metatron's background (since they're considered twin brothers). As months went by and I debated which angels would make up the final twelve for this book, I kept coming across Sandalphon—even to the point of one of my angel books falling on the floor and flipping open to the entry under his name. With a sigh of frustration, I surrendered and figured I'd save him for last, unsure if he would even come if I called him in for an interview.

One night, as I was finishing up a draft of this book, I sat and gazed at Sandalphon's name—forever, it seemed like. Then I set the book aside and looked heavenward. "Sandalphon, if you want in, I need to hear from you . . . soon." I stared at the ceiling, then closed my eyes and opened up all the channels I knew to open. Nothing. Fatigued from a long day in front of the computer, I growled, rolled into bed, and went to sleep.

That night, I had a long and very vivid dream about a homeless squatter who lived in an abandoned high-rise somewhere in New York. The dream's setting was Christmastime, even though it was July when the dream occurred. Upon waking, I found myself confused as to who the squatter was and what he meant to me. But a few days later I would discover that it was Sandalphon in disguise—not just foretelling the success of selling my first book, but reminding me that angels can take on the appearance of many things, often to test our hearts and souls and serve as reminders of spiritual lessons we may have forgotten. (If you're interested in reading about the dream, just flip back to the appendix at the end of this book.)

Sandalphon comes into our lives to help us discover our own inner light, our own happiness. He teaches us that no one can be responsible for our happiness but ourselves, and he helps us to reclaim the power we may have given over to others in exchange for happiness. Likewise, he teaches us that we are not responsible for other people's happiness, either. Everyone must come to the realization that she is concurrently the source of her greatest joys and her greatest miseries. Only you alone can control just how deeply into either realm you wish to venture.

True enough—tragedies happen, and triumphs happen, but because we live a scripted life, we have to come to an understanding in our souls that all things have reason, all things have a purpose. We should not allow ourselves to be swept away by the extreme swings of life's pendulum, but instead keep ourselves centered and focused as much as possible on being an embodiment of joy and peace, no matter what comes our way.

How many times have you heard a friend say, "I just want someone who makes me happy" when talking about their ideal relationship? Right from the start, they're searching for the wrong thing. Happiness comes from within, period. No matter how much money you have, what type of job you have, who you're married to, or who you associate with, none of that should impact inner joy, inner peace. If it does, it's time for a change—and the first place to make those changes is within your soul. Don't be afraid to ask Sandalphon exactly what changes need to be made. Just know that he may give you answers you might not want to hear. In this, you have to have faith in his guidance and know that regardless of what choices you make, regardless of their consequences, everything that happens to you is for your spiritual growth.

One of the first things Sandalphon offers us, to help clear our minds for angelic guidance, is to make time for ourselves to be who we truly are—children of God. Go out and play! Find something fun to do. See a movie, go to the park, draw on your sidewalk with chalk, do whatever puts a smile on your face. In other words, allow your spirit to be free. Whether it's a game of checkers with the kids, a pillow fight with the spouse, or a game of Candy Land by yourself, get into what you're doing. Be in the moment, and allow it to bring to the fore every ounce of life-giving joy and fulfillment there is to be had. It'll be exactly what you need to uplift your soul to the vibration of the angels—where you can hear them clearly and interact with them without trepidation. Remember, you're much more receptive when you go to them in joy than when you go to them in a crisis.

Another thing that Sandalphon brought to my attention, especially during the latter part of this project, was music and how useful it can be when it comes to altering moods. Additionally, if you have issues troubling your heart and you're asking the angels for guidance, turn on the radio. Listen to the music, listen to the lyrics. There'll be a message waiting in there for you that will give you food for thought or even inspire you to take some sort of action to bring about change in your life.

While I was writing this book, I ran into a typical rut: "Why bother? Why am I doing this and wasting my time?" Sandalphon and Michael both showed up, and Michael nudged me toward the classic disco station on satellite radio that afternoon. I sat listening to the upbeat music with a sour face, not really being moved by it . . . until. After about the third or fourth selection, I noticed a link between the songs, beyond the heavy snare drums, hand claps, and violins. Each and every song, for about eight songs straight, had either "heaven" or "angel" in its title. I noticed this trend by the time "Heaven Knows" by Donna Summer came on. I just looked up at the ceiling and threw up my arms in surrender.

"All right, I'll finish it!" I would like to say I got a lot of writing done that night, but I was laughing too hard at Michael and Sandalphon gettin' down and boogyin' their tails off.

Eventually, I got back to work, but then I realized how I needed that break—just for a few minutes—to get my mind and spirit back on the same page. That's when Sandalphon comes to us, to show us the delicate balance between work and play. Work may put food on the table, but play puts laughter in your soul. We should honor both realms equally.

> *Laughter is the tonic, the relief, the surcease for pain.*
> —CHARLIE CHAPLIN

ARCHANGEL

AZRAEL

AN INTERCESSOR

Azrael holds in his hands the fate of all,
including us angels. Michael is toast.

—ARCHANGEL SANDALPHON

———————

MEANING OF NAME: God helps.

TRIVIA: Commonly associated with the Grim Reaper, Azrael has been depicted in more Hollywood films than all of his archangel brothers put together.

MESSAGE TO THE CONTEMPORARY WORLD: To eliminate the fear of death, one must first eliminate the desire to control life. Death is not a call to judgment. It is merely a call home.

PATRON ANGEL (TRADITIONALLY) OF: Death, the dying and the dead, caretakers, morticians; also watches over pallbearers to secure their steps in a procession.

PATRON ANGEL (CURRENTLY) OF: The above, plus grief counselors, funeral home directors.

RULER OF: Saturday (Saturn); co-rules with Cassiel.

HEAVENLY ASSIGNMENT: While any angel or choir of angels can appear at our moment of transition from this existence to the next, humans who fight and struggle in fear of the unknown will be ushered to the other side by the powerful Azrael.

DEMEANOR WHEN ON THE JOB: For the most part, Azrael is kind, gentle, and loving. It is only because he attends those refusing to let this existence go that such a gruesome stigma follows him.

DEMEANOR WHEN AT PLAY: Azrael has a fondness for children because they are so accepting of their fate. He can be quite a universal showman, and enjoys coaxing innocent giggles and starry-eyed gazes of wonder from children.

HUMAN ACCOMPLISHMENTS MOST PROUD OF: He doesn't bother to pay much attention. "All things are transient and never last very long."

BACK IN THE DAY, HE LIKED: Staying in his mansion or visiting the other archangels. "There was a time when humans were much more accepting of their transition and I wasn't called upon nearly as much as I am now."

TODAY, HE ENJOYS: Anyone who lovingly embraces him upon first meeting. (Usually he's dragging souls off kicking and screaming.)

PET PEEVE: Nothing. Humans are what they are.

HOPE FOR THE WORLD (SERIOUS): Funerals should focus more on actually celebrating the life of an individual than mourning their loss.

HOPE FOR THE WORLD (WHIMSICAL): With the above said, "every reception should have a karaoke machine and no one gets out until he has made a complete fool of himself. Laughter is the most healing element of all; its sound resonates throughout the universe."

IF HE HAD AN ASTROLOGICAL SIGN, IT WOULD BE: Pisces.

ELEMENTS: Nothing in particular.

GEMSTONES WITH SIMILAR VIBRATION: Black tourmaline (diffuses fear for ease of transitions).

FAVORITE SEASON(S): Winter.

ANIMAL TOTEM(S): Moth/butterfly, dragon, crow, raven.

WING COLOR: Black with dove-gray speckles.

FAVORITE ATTIRE: Black billowing robes, scythe.

FAVORITE COLOR(S): No preference.

FAVORITE FOOD(S): Chocolate, sweets.

FAVORITE MUSIC: All types.

IDEAL DATE: An old silent film at the cinema with a bucket of popcorn (heavy butter), followed by dinner at the best mom-and-pop pizzeria in town. Whatever you do, don't ask "How's work going?"

ASCENDED MASTERS AND BENEVOLENT SPIRIT TEACHERS WITH SIMILAR ENERGY SIGNATURES: Charon, Enma, Kali, Yama.

NOTABLE PEOPLE WITH SIMILAR VIBRATION: They probably wouldn't feel comfortable being listed here.

FAVORITE CONTEMPORARY FICTIONAL CHARACTERS: Himself in any media, but he's most fond of his portrayal in *Bill and Ted's Excellent Adventure: Bogus Adventure*, as well as in *Family Guy* episodes and other parodies in pop culture.

USUALLY ARRIVES IN YOUR LIFE: When you are struggling with any notion of death, be it your own or that of someone you know or love. Azrael is not to be feared, but to be embraced as a guide to lead us from one existence to the next. He doesn't just show up when death is approaching; he also comes to us to allay our fears of death when it is still so far away. Azrael once told me, "Chantel, you are going to be here for quite a while still, and who better to give you that news than the Angel of Death?" He said it with a wink, an impish smirk, and an elbow in my ribs that certainly contradicted his usual malevolent depiction.

AZRAEL'S MANSION

I've saved the grandest mansion for last. *What, it's grander than Michael's?* Yes, indeed. Azrael's mansion sits above all the other archangel mansions, at the top of the dome that houses these elaborate spaces. At first, the doorway to Azrael's mansion confused me a bit. When I reached the top of the dome, there was an inconspicuous hatch that led me to think there was nothing but attic space beyond. I know, dumb thought, but when I see a hatch at the top of a passageway, my first thought is storage space. I can't help it; I'm a clutter-bug.

It took both hands and a lot of strength to push the door open. When I poked my head through, all I saw was darkness.

"Attic, I knew it." I groaned with disappointment. But then I gazed directly up and nearly lost my balance—I was swept away by a vision astronauts would be envious of.

When Leonardo DiCaprio exclaimed, "I'm the king of the world!" in the blockbuster film *Titanic*, I'm sure Azrael chortled a bit, for the Archangel of Death's mansion is a panoramic view of the universe into infinity. There are no palaces, no pillars of limestone, no statues of granite, nothing but stars and planets and swirling, pulsating clouds of brilliant colors against a sea of black. It is a god's-eye view of existence, and there are no words in any language that can describe the sheer size and beauty of what I beheld.

"My brothers get up here more often than I do." Azrael startled me as he fluidly emerged from the hatch to join me for a bit of stargazing. "Cassiel lets the dragons out to romp around and play." He said this as casually as if he were talking about two cocker spaniels. I sat down beside him and leaned against his tall frame. I was utterly speechless, and didn't know what to say or if I should say anything at such a profound moment. But, to my chagrin, Azrael broke the silence and noted that I was viewing just a fraction of all there was to see—no human eye could ever behold the full majesty and grandness of Creation.

As I sat there, meditating on the stars and nebulas, planets and clouds of dust, I thought it was a bit disconcerting that the Angel of Death was the one granted the privilege of calling this spot his mansion; he could sit like a silent sentinel, watching time and Creation unfold. After all, wasn't he a destroyer of sorts? Was he watching the galaxies he would take out next? I'm sure he heard my thoughts, since he put his hand on my shoulder and softly spoke:

"We are all made of energy, Chantel, energy that can never be destroyed, only transformed and redistributed. Humans may see me as a harbinger of death, but I am merely a conduit through which they must go to get to their next state of existence. That's all." He looked at me with saddened eyes and I had to reach up to pat his shoulder.

"Well, if it's all the same to you, Azrael, I'd like you to serve as a conduit through which I become a size two with a metabolism that won't quit."

"I like you, Chantel." He chuckled back at me.

"Good. Does this buy me a few more years on my life script, since we're all chummy-like?"

"Don't push it."

What would Azrael be if he were human?
The top-billed performer in a hit Broadway show.
Shh, don't tell him I told you that.
—ARCHANGEL MICHAEL

AZRAEL MANIFEST

Many of my clients know that I use "reverse angel-neering." As discussed earlier, it means that I'll only research an angel once he/she has established contact with me. But it doesn't always happen that way. Sometimes I'll get a few clues from external sources, which tell me to look into a particular angel or ascended master beforehand. This was the case for Archangel Azrael.

It should come as no surprise that for nearly a decade working with the archangels, Archangel Azrael (also known as the Angel of Death in Islamic and Judaic lore) was an angel I never wanted to meet. Like so many other people, I had an unspoken fear of the Angel of Death; I always wondered if it would mean that my time was up if I crossed his path. Well, I've met the Angel of Death and I'm still here, able to write about it.

It all started when a client asked me, quite matter-of-factly, if I had ever seen the Angel of Death in a client consultation.

I chuckled nervously and told her, "No, and I don't ever want to."

The question stayed with me long after the discussion, and when I got home, I was drawn to researching Azrael's lore. I was

already informally familiar with him, having gleaned knowledge from books during my angst-filled teenage years. But as
an adult, I developed a much healthier respect for death. After
all, logistically speaking, I'm much closer to it now than I was
fifteen years ago, right?

All night, before doing any serious research on Azrael, I
actually chanted, "Ignorance is bliss." Then, with hesitant and
trembling hands, I went to my old stomping grounds of the early
1990s. Back before the Internet and blogging, there were fanzines
and pen pals. That's how I discovered, and later visited, the Azrael
Project in New Orleans (they've relocated since Hurricane Ka-
trina). I was first introduced to the dark angel in that big purple
house on Magazine Street, and so it was only natural that I return
to the Project (this time via the Internet) to refamiliarize myself
with him. What I'd thought was cool during my teenage years
spooked the daylights out of me that night. I quickly turned to
my collection of angel books for cross-reference and it was then,
in the midst of quiet study, that I felt the atmosphere in the room
change. The air felt cooler, heavier. I ignored the phenomenon,
thinking it was my imagination. Well, I was hoping, anyhow.

Then I felt a hand on my right shoulder. I froze and held
my breath.

Azrael appeared by my side. His complexion was like black
slate, his skin like velvet. He looked at me with translucent gray
eyes—tender gray eyes. Needless to say, I was nervous, but

he assuaged my fears with one statement: "Chantel, you need never fear me."

I exhaled and let my shoulders relax. From that point on we talked about his brothers the archangels, and my job of working with them. His presence was warm and fatherly. Yes, he wore black robes, but they were stunning as they flowed around him like liquid obsidian; and yes, he brought his scythe with him, but he was hardly frightening. If anything, I thought the scythe was interesting and attractive.

Anyhow, Azrael had a gentle, sotto voce sense of humor, and his smile was one of the handsomest smiles I've ever seen. Overall, my talk with him was relaxing and insightful. And I was relieved to know that my time was not up … yet.

Remember, fear is dispelled by experience and wisdom. Like many of you, I too had a fear of Azrael, but once I got to know him, I realized that Heaven has appointed him a task and he is as close to God as all the other archangels are. In fact, some sources say that Azrael not only holds the fate of humans in his hands, but the fate of his angelic brothers, too. Azrael confirmed this with me when we spoke.

I think that because it is natural for humans to fear the Unknown, and therefore death, we naturally fear the one who brings death to us. This fear is unfounded. Azrael is an unbiased, compassionate being whose purpose is to guide us to the other side when our time comes. He is not someone to fear,

but someone to cling to—to embrace at that final moment. He is strong, protective, and wise, deserving much more esteem than he's gotten over the centuries.

Maybe in the new millennium, humans will shed their fear of death and instead accept it as a part of life, facing it with the knowing that we are eternal beings. Our souls are comprised of the same energy that flows through the cosmos. Energy cannot be destroyed—it can only transform. Does an ice cube fear turning to liquid? Does water fear turning into air? To be quite honest, of course, I don't know whether human transformation from this existence to the next is as easy as an ice cube melting on the kitchen counter. I've been told that it is as simple as going to sleep—but I'm not yet ready to test that theory.

> *Death and love are the two wings*
> *that bear the good man to heaven.*
> —MICHELANGELO

Appendix

A Dream…Christmas in July

Here follows my dream of Sandalphon in disguise, just days before we formally met:

I stood outside an abandoned apartment building, gazing up at many stories of broken windows. The wind was gusting by, bringing with it a wintry chill, and I pulled the collar of my wool coat up around my chin. I didn't know how I got there. I felt like I had been suddenly beamed down to the spot from the Starship Enterprise. I spun around, hoping to find something familiar, but was only greeted by a deserted and dilapidated cityscape. More cold than apprehensive, I stepped into the foyer of the abandoned building and squirmed past cobwebs and spiders dangling from the ceiling. Ick.

The building was well past its prime, with boarded windows and doors hanging from the hinges, but I was compelled to explore anyway.

So I did—up a dusty marble staircase. As I ascended, I noticed that the sun was setting, and by time I got to what looked like an atrium on the top floor, nighttime had shrouded the building and I was walking by the grace of faint blue moonlight.

A gust of wind startled me. I looked up. The atrium's skylight was broken—my, how the stars shone against the black sky!

"Hey, you." The voice came from nowhere. I gazed across the atrium into the dense shadows. I wasn't afraid, but I wasn't about to move, either. I decided that standing close to the exit was the best thing to do.

"Who's there?" I called back, only to be answered by the sound of a striking match. The flame illuminated a corner across the room and touched the wicks of several candles, giving the atrium a warm amber glow. A shadowy figure lifted up a large white pillar and turned to me. He was a young man, no older than twenty or so, with deep, absorbing eyes and a soft smile.

"It's me," he chirped. I couldn't help but notice the smudges of grime on his face, his unkempt hair, his baggy, tattered clothing.

"Hello, me. You're squatting in the worst place. The draft is kinda harsh, don't you think?" I began to approach him.

"Are you kidding? Look at the view!" He gestured up to the sky, and I offered a light chuckle. I looked up again, and could not remember a time in my life when I had seen stars so bright. With a frosty sigh, I tucked my hands in my pockets and casually approached the youth. He seemed harmless enough.

245

"So, this is home?" I'd barely gotten the words out when I stepped on a large, dusty and matted area rug. My foot sank into a hole beneath it and I stumbled forward. But the fall wasn't broken by the floor. Cradled in the rug, I fell through a massive gap and screamed all the way down. I hit another floor, only to crash through the rotted floorboards. Confined by the carpeting and paralyzed with panic, I plummeted; and when it all stopped, I could barely catch my breath. Still, I was cradled in the rug and I was swaying. I wasn't on solid ground, and I feared that my fall wasn't yet over.

"Hey, you okay down there?" I heard the man call to me. I was face down in the musty carpet and couldn't see a thing.

"NO!" My cries were muffled and I tried to turn over to keep from suffocating.

"Don't struggle! I'll pull you up!" And so he did, although it seemed like it took forever. He helped me back up into the atrium and brushed off my coat. Furious, I swatted back at him to fend him off.

"Why didn't you tell me there was a hole in the floor!" I shrieked.

"You lived, didn't you? Wow, seven stories. Lucky you didn't even hit the bottom floor. It's marble and doesn't give as well as wood."

I was incensed, but winded and too shaken up to argue with him. I backed away from the hole and went to sit in a

corner. Trembling, I fell silent and gazed at the crater. It was enormous, leaving less than a yard of creaky floorboards that ran around the perimeter of the room. Now big enough to swallow a luxury sedan, it wasn't just a hole. The entire floor of the room was gone!

"I could've died." My voice broke as tears of shock burned my eyes. Then I looked up at him. "You tried to kill me!"

"Nonsense. I just saved you! What do you mean, tried to kill you? Pshaw." He was placing the rug back over the hole as if nothing ever happened. "Just walk around the edges of the room next time. You'll be all right."

"Gee, thanks," I scoffed and got my breath back. My legs stopped shaking enough for me to stand, and I began to skim the edges of the room toward the exit.

"I'm quite intelligent, you know. Of course, no one would know that just by looking at me," he mumbled. I was hardly in a sympathetic mood. I nodded politely and continued slinking along the wall like a ninja spy.

"No. Don't go. I have something for you." His hands were up in protest and he went to dig through a pile of junk in a corner. I was finally near the stairwell, confident that he couldn't negotiate the wall fast enough to catch up to me, but a floorboard creaked under my foot and I froze.

"Here!" He was kitty-corner from me, across the room—across the crater that the rug covered. He started toward me.

"What are you doing?" I put my hands up in protest, hoping to stop him from crossing the rug, but when he did, it was solid beneath as he padded heavily upon it. Stupefied, I could only gaze at his feet. Seconds later, my attention was diverted as he held out his hand to me. In it was a gold and pearl broach in the shape of an angel.

"This is yours. I make these, but no one seems to like them." He took my hand and gently placed the broach in my palm. The gold shone brightly and the saltwater pearls radiated the iridescent colors of the sea. I held it up to view it in the flickering candlelight.

"Wow, it's beautiful. Thank you." Even in a dream, I'm a sucker for trinkets.

"I'm glad you like it. Most people discard them. I'll trust you won't."

"Oh. Um. No...but uh, this one is...well, it's dented right here." How ungrateful could I be?

"No, it's not."

"Yeah, right here." I showed it to him as I held it up in the light.

"Where? There's no dent." He insisted.

"Right here, look. The frame's bent." I pointed to the angel's gold robe where there was indeed an indentation.

"Look at it again." He dismissed me and headed back to the other side of the room, across the carpet. Flustered, I gazed at the broach again, only to realize the dent was actually a part of the angel's wing—a hidden wing. I grinned at the optical illusion and pinned the broach on my lapel.

I descended the staircase sheepishly, but when I got to the bottom floor of the building, it wasn't an abandoned apartment building anymore, but a bustling office building. Caught off guard, I felt a bit awkward, and I snuck out the front of the building only to find myself standing on the snow-covered streets of a bustling metropolis. A horse-drawn carriage went by, jingling, and traffic sped along.

"New York? What the . . . " I spun around several times in disbelief. I had never visited New York in my life.

Look down. I heard the voice in my head. I looked down at the icy pavement to find another gold angel pin that matched the one just given to me. I looked around, silently waving the jewelry to see if anyone would claim it. The doorman regarded me a moment and then looked away as if to say, *Humph, tourists.*

I smiled as I tucked the pin in my pocket. Then I began to walk away, but I heard the voice again. *Look down.* I stopped and looked down to find another pin! I picked it up and stood there on the cold sidewalk, unsure what to do or think.

Look up.

And I did, up to the top floor of what was again the abandoned apartment building. The young man stood in the window, holding his candle. He made a gesture to me to stand still, and he disappeared from the window a moment. Wind gusted by, bringing with it a flurry of snow, but it didn't break my attention—curiosity held me to the spot.

Within seconds, the youth returned to the window—but looked like he was struggling, wrestling, with two snakes! I squinted as I watched the drama unfold, only to be startled by an explosion of light—bright, flickering Christmas lights. I then saw that he was struggling with two electrical extension cords. He dropped them in seeming frustration, grabbed a Santa Claus hat, and put it on his head. He then threw his arms open as if to say *ta-da!* I chuckled at his antics and shrugged, unsure what to make of the over-the-top display that now lit up the roof of the building, as well as the monstrous Christmas tree that stood in the window.

And as if that weren't impressive enough, he opened the window and nudged something that was dangling from the roof. A bright, neon sign flickered on that read, *Merry Christmas, Chantel*.

"It's July!" I laughed hysterically up at him.

"Wha ... ?" he bellowed as he cupped his ear.

"It's July. It's not Christmas!"

He looked around and then up to the sky. "It's snowing!"

"I'm dreaming!"

"Yes, you are. But Merry Christmas anyhow!"

When I woke up, I was overcome with laughter and tears. It was a bittersweet moment, especially since my Christmases are spent more in reflection than festivities. Both Mom and Dad have passed on, and the holiday tends to go by quietly. I pondered the dream of the homeless youth all morning, trying to understand what it meant. I thought it might be one of those dreams that have to be digested over time, but I wondered if it was an angel's unique way of connecting with me—through a dream I had to decipher like the great kings of the Bible did (Nebuchadnezzar and Daniel the Prophet come to mind). I wondered if it was Sandalphon—who I hadn't yet interviewed, who was holding up the proverbial train of me finishing my book.

Exactly three days later, on my birthday, I heard from a publisher who was interested in this manuscript. Merry Christmas, indeed.

But even after the dream and the unexpected surprise, I still wasn't compelled to write about Sandalphon. I figured well, if it had been him in the dream, it was a grand entrance to be sure—but not having formally met him, I had little to go on. Or so I thought.

A few nights later I sat at my computer, even more disgruntled with Sandalphon now that I had a real deadline. I still hadn't heard from him; in fact, all angelic communication seemed to go dead right when I began panicking about the book's completion. Here I finally had a publisher willing to look at the manuscript, and one of the archangels decided to go MIA. One might think that I should have looked for another angel to take Sandalphon's place, but after the barrage of signs that I'd received confirming that he indeed was to be the twelfth angel, I didn't dare go looking for an understudy. So I waited.

Welcome to my life with the angels.

Still, I'm human; my patience only lasts so long. Even after all the research I'd done on him (because he's hard to miss when researching his brother Metatron), it wasn't enough. I needed to meet him, talk with him, and see the spirit behind the name. As days went by, my frustration grew, and I was a breath away from giving up on the elusive angel and—to my chagrin—the entire project. It was then that a dear friend showed up, shocking the daylights out of me.

"Dean, heya." I beamed as my muse appeared. Dean and I had hooked up a few Christmases ago when I had set my sights on working on a bit of fiction. I didn't know exactly where this spirit guide had come from, but he was fun, entertaining, and had a Charlie Chaplin flair to him. Unfortunately, he and I spent more time talking about games, music, and old movies than we did writing. But hey, what are friends for? In a strange way, I sort of felt like I was Calvin and he was Hobbes. Time passed quickly whenever he showed up, and we always found ourselves in stitches over one thing or another.

Unfortunately, I was hardly in a laughing mood that night when he appeared, since I was fuming and ready to kick Sandalphon's angelic hinny to the curb.

"What's the matter?" He peered at my computer screen while sucking on a lollipop.

"I got this book to finish. I've got one last angel to add. I think he showed up in this dream a few nights ago, and I've tried to connect with him, but I'm getting dead air. He won't talk to me!"

"Well, who?" Those big, inquisitive eyes looked up at me.

"Sandalphon! Metatron's brother." I pushed back from the computer.

"I'm here." My spirit guide said innocently.

"What?" I sat up and looked at him. "You're not Sandalphon! Your name is Dean!"

"No. You just started calling me Dean."

"Well, you look like a Dean! Why didn't you say something?"

"Hey, you never asked, and you were happy calling me Dean." He shrugged. "Let's do this." He tapped his lollipop on the keyboard and sat back in the chair, kicking up his feet. He gave a tug to his pageboy cap. "What'cha wanna know?"

"Was that you in the dream?" I turned to him, my hand pressed firmly to my hip to keep it from lunging at the angel's throat.

"Yeap. I wanted to be the first one to congratulate you on the book."

I finally exploded with emotions that I had kept pinned down for days. Here was my opportunity of a lifetime, and he wanted to play charades? "The boy in the dream didn't look anything like you. You could have thrown me a clue or two as to who you were!" I glowered at him and then turned back to my computer. My poor mouse took a serious beating as I firmly clicked around, opening a new document for the interview.

"Someone brings you a gift and you complain about the gift wrap?" Sandalphon's brows knitted together as he spoke softly. I doubt his big, brown eyes could scare a gnat, but I saw a tincture of chastisement in his gaze and I sighed in resignation. With a single glance and turn of a phrase, he had me awash in guilt.

"Look, I'm sorry. It's just that I'm behind schedule with this project. It should have been finished days ago." I tried to defend my feelings, albeit sheepishly.

He gently placed his hand upon my shoulder, gave it a squeeze, and then leaned forward, propping his chin on my shoulder so he could whisper in my ear. "Chantel, when will you ever learn that everything happens exactly when it's supposed to? There are no such words as 'early' or 'late' in the angel vocabulary. We are, and always will be, right on time. Smile, it's Christmas."

He gave me a soft nudge and leaned back. I couldn't help but cast a sarcastic glance at my window, where the hot July sun was pouring in. But then I suddenly remembered my mother's words from when I was a child: "Because life is the most precious gift God gives us, every day we live is Christmas."

BIBLIOGRAPHY

Braden, Gregg. *The Divine Matrix*. Carlsbad, CA: Hay House, 2006.

Davidson, Gustav. *A Dictionary of Angels: Including the Fallen Angels*. New York: The Free Press, 1967.

De Chardin, Teilhard. *The Phenomenon of Man*. New York: Harper Collins, 1959.

Embree, Ainslee. *Sources of Indian Tradition*. New York: Columbia University Press, 1988.

Guiley, Rosemary. *The Encyclopedia of Saints*. New York: Checkmark Books, 2001.

Holy Bible. Authorized King James Version. Grand Rapids, MI: World Bible Publishers, 1989.

Keel, Othmar. *Gods, Goddesses, and Images of God*. London: T&T Clark Publishers, 2001.

Lewis, James R., and Evelyn Dorothy Oliver. *Angels A to Z*. Canton, MI: Visible Ink Press, 2002.

Myss, Caroline. *Anatomy of the Spirit*. New York: Three Rivers Press, 1996.

RavenWolf, Silver. *Angels: Companions in Magick*. St. Paul, MN: Llewellyn Publications, 1996.

Simpson, Liz. *The Book of Chakra Healing*. New York: Sterling Publishing, 1999.

Taylor, Terry Lynn. *Messengers of Light: The Angels' Guide to Spiritual Growth*. Tiburon, CA: H. J. Kramer, Inc., 1990.

Turner, Judith. *The Hidden World of Birthdays*. New York: Firestone, 1999.

Virtue, Doreen. *Archangels & Ascended Masters*. Carlsbad, CA: Hay House Inc., 2003.

Webster's Third New International Dictionary, Unabridged. Merriam-Webster, 2002.

OTHER SOURCES

The Azrael Project™ Online,
http://www.westgatenecromantic.com